Marriage
911

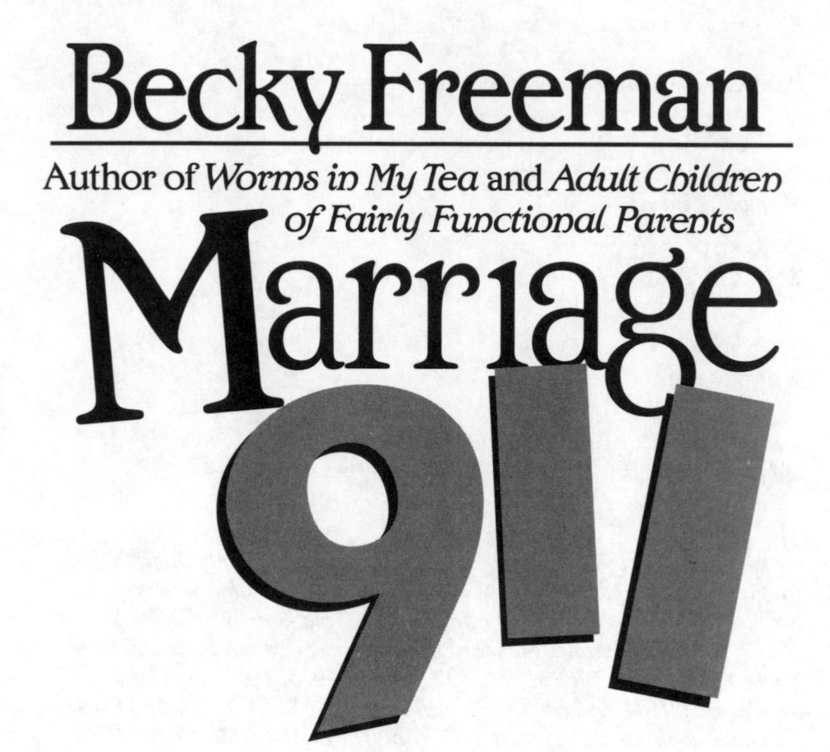

Becky Freeman

Author of *Worms in My Tea* and *Adult Children of Fairly Functional Parents*

Marriage 911

Nashville, Tennessee

Printed in the United States of America

Published by:
Broadman & Holman Publishers
Nashville, Tennessee

Designed by:
Steven Boyd

4261-78
0-8054-6178-7

Dewey Decimal Classification: 306.872
Subject Heading: MARRIAGE \ FAMILY
Library of Congress Card Catalog Number: 95-10921

Library of Congress Cataloging-in-Publication Data
Freeman, Becky
Marriage 911 / Becky Freeman
p. cm.
ISBN 0-8054-6178-7 (pbk.)
1. Marriage—United States. I. Title.
HQ734.F748 1996
306.81—dc20

95-10921
CIP

00 99 98 97 96 5 4 3 2 1

With love, to Scott—
for still wanting to grow up with me.

Contents

Acknowledgments

Who would have thought she would have taken me seriously? I was definitely writing with tongue (or should I say *pen?*) planted firmly in cheek. But here was my editor, Vicki Crumpton, on the other end of the phone, and she sounded serious.

"Becky," she said, "how about giving me a proposal for that authoritative/marriage self-help book? You know, the one you mentioned in *Worms in My Tea*—the one called *Our Marriage Is Better and We Still Haven't Figured Out Exactly Why.*"

"Well," I laughed, "first of all, you know I was just joking around. And second, I'm anything but authoritative. I'm not even *that* great at helping myself. I still need lots of people supporting me."

"Exactly—that's why I think *you* should write this. It would be fun."

I decided not to ask, "For whom?" I was both thrilled and terrified. The truth? I still am.

As things moved along we decided it might be best to choose a less complicated title. Little did any of us realize how complicated it would be to come up with a less complicated title. I only know that at one time we were all ready to call this book, *We Can't Think of a Good Title, So You Make One Up*. Vicki came to the rescue with her brainstorm, *Marriage 911*, just in the nick of time. I love it.

So a special thank you, Vicki, Colyer Robison, and Greg Webster—and all my other friends and team players at Broadman & Holman—for helping to pull it off. It hasn't always been easy, but with you guys, it's always been a hoot.

There's another special lady to whom I owe a heartful of thanks for helping to make this book a reality.

I must admit, however, that I didn't completely pull this off alone. You see, the manuscript was complete, but something was missing—some pieces to the puzzle were out of place. So a week before my deadline, I flew home to my mother's writing nest and chirped, "Help!" With the skill of a plastic surgeon, she knew right away exactly where to nip and where to tuck. She has a gift for this, pure and simple.

So even though this was not a co-written project, fans of my mother (Ruthie Arnold) will still find pieces of her tucked into scenes—places where she spiced up a passage, or put pieces in more logical order, or cleaned out excess words. She continues to help me grow in this difficult, glorious, nebulous craft called writing, just as she continues to help me grow in this difficult, glorious, nebulous thing called life. On both accounts I'm learning from the best. So thank you, Mother. I love you more than I can say. (And I will help you clean out the garage next week—I promise!)

To Mary Rusch, my dear friend—We've been through it all, haven't we? How grateful I am for your insightful critique, your constant encouragement, and your never-ending sense of fun.

To Melissa Gantt—You came into my life just when I needed a friend. Thanks for your cheerleading and wonderful input.

To Dean Dykstra—Thank you for offering to read this manuscript and for the honest, excellent suggestions. I took them to heart and I believe it made a tremendous difference in the final product.

To Mike Hyatt—thanks for your assistance with the business end of this project so I could have more freedom to concentrate on the fun part.

And last, but not least, to my precious, precious husband, Scott—We each take our share of ribbing in these pages, but you've always had the wonderful ability to *laugh* at "us." Our souls, sometimes, are laid bare in these pages—but you've always had the wonderful ability to be open about "us." You didn't leave me alone on some writing limb; you shared in the process and helped make this book better reflect some of who we really are. And as peculiar as our "us-ness" is, I love it.

So thank you, My Love, for being there.

INTRODUCTION

Pull yerself up a chair and set a spell

We're on vacation now, at probably my most favorite place in the whole world—the Florida Coastline. I've had the exquisite pleasure of two hours alone on the beach. Alone, that is, except for my icy cold fruit drink, a gentle ocean breeze, the faint echo of waves splashing the shore, a pen, and a notebook. What more could a body ask for? Maybe a good book. Maybe a good friend. Yeah, that's it. A good friend.

Since there is the possibility that you and I might become friends by the time we finish this book, may I invite you to curl up and get comfy? And don't forget to pour yourself a cup of soothing hot tea or rich coffee.

For the bulk of our time together, shall we toss around the topic of marriage? After all, that is what the title on the cover portends. But before I get too personal, I'd like to preface what is to come with a few pre-book thoughts.

I've agonized over exactly what to say, how to put into words what Scott and I have discovered and are learning daily. Marriage is complicated because people are complicated. Some of us couples do seem a bit more befuddled than others, I must admit. If there were a simple formula for success, believe me, we'd have found it by now. I've certainly done my research. All I know is that our marriage is better now than it has ever been, but I'm still hard-pressed to say exactly why. Perhaps in the process of writing, as is so often the case for me, I'll begin to see it all more clearly.

At this point, all I've got are these fragments floating around in my head of what has worked for us—but I think they are significant fragments. And though our relationship is for the most part good and solid, there are days when I've moaned, "Oh, shoot. I don't know how to make a relationship work. Who do I think I am to write a book about marriage anyway?"

I can relate to Erma Bombeck's conclusion in her latest book, *A Marriage Made in Heaven or Too Tired for an Affair*. She wrote, "I wanted to end this book with a wise and wonderful statement on how marriages work. I don't have a clue."[1]

But at my lowest points, just before I pick up the phone to call the publisher to inform them that I am not the right person for this project after all, Scott gently reminds me, "Becky, this isn't supposed to be a how-to book on marriage."

Oh, yeah, I think to myself, *That's right!* and I relax.

It's only our story—and not even the whole story because I can't possibly write everything. There are things between my husband and me that are held sacred and private. And some incidents are forgiven and forgotten and never to be dug up again, even for the sake of an intriguing book. Still, our marriage never seems lacking in plenty of material we can share.

Scott also frequently issues another reminder. "Becky, you've got to write this book in the genre where our marriage, for the most part, belongs—on the humor shelf." I frown, but I must admit he's absolutely right.

Since neither Scott nor I appear to have a shred of hope of being nominated for sainthood, I will be sharing with you the selected few fragments we have been able—by the grace of

God—to apply now and then. I have no formulas for you, no miracles or surefire twelve-step programs between these pages. Instead, I'll offer glimpses into a real-life marriage in the works. Perhaps you will come away saying, "Whew. At least we aren't as crazy as that couple. Things are better in my relationship than I thought!" Or you may say, "Well, how about that? We aren't the only couple in America whose relationship sometimes feels like a roller coaster out of control."

But remember, I'm taking the risk of being vulnerable here by opening the curtain on scenes from selected "Days of Our Lives." So will you read with a kind heart, please? In turn, I'm praying as I write that my words might touch some husband or wife, that our stories might be used to encourage some couple hanging on by a thread to "hangeth thou in there," as Kay Arthur is fond of saying. At the very least, I hope we both might come to the end of this book saying, "A good time was had by all."

And if, by chance, I happen to touch your heart, I'll be keeping the Italian Cappuccino fresh and hot for our next visit together.

Becky Freeman
Destin, Florida

ONE

Romance, window dressing, and pickled pigs' feet

I am not, by any stretch of the imagination, what you would call a naturally wild and wanton woman. But I'd been married fifteen years, and I felt our marriage needed a little—spice.

It all began with a romantic suggestion I gleaned from a book titled *Light His Fire*. The author, Ellen Kriedman, suggests that wives use their ingenuity to come up with imaginative ways to have fun seducing their mate. The book assured me that, done properly, this technique should fire up the I-feel-a-chill-in-the-air times most couples experience at some point in their relationship.

Nothing new here, really. Ever since the days when perky Mrs. Marabel Morgan first suggested we Christian women greet our husbands at the door dressed in plastic wrap and/or an apron, we wives have spent a couple of decades trying to outdo the Total Woman. Personally, I have come to the conclusion that such efforts leave me feeling more like a Totaled Woman. Not that I hadn't given wild and creative tactics my best shot, mind you.

One night as I stepped out of the shower wrapped in a towel, I spied the lights of Scott's pickup in the driveway of our home. Our closest neighbors were raccoons and possums, so I didn't worry about the undraped window overlooking the drive. Suddenly I could almost hear Dr. Kriedman whispering in my ear.

Why not? After all, you're married to the guy. Be playful! Be sexy! Have some fun with your man!

So I dropped the towel and stood there in front of the window wearing nothing but my best seductive smile. As it happened, Scott was not alone. This night he had with him our good friend Gary, husband of my dear friend Mary. As the two men walked casually toward the house (I learned later), Scott glanced toward the window, returned for a second to his conversation with Gary, and then jerked his head back toward the window, his eyes wide, his mouth agape. He then alternated between trying to divert Gary's eyes from our bedroom window and gesturing frantically for me to run for cover.

Lamentably, though it is easy to see *into* a lighted home from the dark, it is quite difficult for the one standing inside the house to see *out* into the dark. Because of this phenomenon, I imagined Scott must surely be whooping it up out there in the night air. I even thought I heard him egging me on with playful wolf whistles. Later I would discover the "whistles" were actually high-pitched sounds made by Scott's vocal chords desperately searching for the natural range of his voice. In any case, I simply responded to what I had assumed was my husband's enthusiastic reaction.

Finally, having safely escorted Gary into the kitchen, Scott breathed a sigh of relief and began to relax. Observing that nothing could undo the damage that had already been done, my husband nonchalantly poked his head into the bedroom.

"Hi, Hon," he said casually, "Gary's with me."

My screams, I'm sure, awakened every possum and raccoon in nearby trees. I thought I would die. My thoughts were a frenzy. *I've* just flashed my best friend's husband! It doesn't get any worse than this. Of all the stupid antics . . . this absolutely tops the list! I vowed to avoid Gary for the rest of my life. I couldn't possibly face him again without dissolving into a puddle of shame and embarrassment.

The next morning, Mary, Gary's wife, called bright and early. "Becky," she said brightly, "Gary asked me to deliver a message to you." Switching to a deep French accent she went on, "He says to tell you 'Becky, jou look mahvahlous.'"

When the laughter finally began to clear on her end of the line, Mary added, "And, hey, I just want you to know, since I've been feeling a bit under the weather lately, this probably *made* his week."

Because they both had a great sense of humor, we all recovered fairly quickly. With time and understanding, I am now able to hold a normal conversation with Gary without benefit of a paper bag over my head.

The Window Story has already made its way through our small town, down grocery store aisles, across neighborhood fences, into most of our fellow parishioners' ears between services, and is probably being translated into several foreign languages. My best friends, and even my husband, love to tell it at appropriate gatherings when conversation drops to a lull.

After that little escapade, one would assume I would have laid to rest any impulse to do something wild and crazy and romantic for at least awhile. One would assume.

Then one evening, feeling rather amorous, I stepped out of the bathtub and noticed a large, yellow, transparent bag hanging over the towel rack—a bag that had been used to cover Scott's dry-cleaned shirts. Viewing all that plastic, I thought I heard voices again. This time it was the Total Woman speaking.

If at first you don't succeed, try, try, again.

Inspired, I draped the mustard-colored wrap around my torso, ingeniously holding it together with a couple of bobby pins I found in the sink. Slinking toward the bedroom where my husband was reclining with a good book, I opened the door with a flourish. He continued to read, so I loudly cleared my throat. He finally glanced up, shook his head as if to clear it, frowned in bewilderment, and scratched his chin. Not quite the reaction I had anticipated. It got worse.

"What have you done to yourself now?" Scott asked sincerely. "You've made your entire body look like one of those supermarket meat trays of pickled pigs' feet!"

I wasn't as crushed as you might expect from that verbal blow to my ego. I had to admit, a last-minute glance in the bathroom mirror had filled me with a few serious doubts. I had gone into this mission knowing its outcome was chancy, at best. But I was no longer in a wild and crazy romantic state of mind, either. As to my pork-minded husband's chances for an evening of love, I have just one thing to say—"That little piggy had none."

The following Fourth of July, this little piggy went to market to shop for the outdoor barbeque we were planning. And guess what I found? A meat tray full of pigs' feet covered with plastic wrap. A wicked smile spread across my face, and I instantly knew what cut of meat my husband would be having for dinner. Did I laugh as I thought of Scott sitting down to a plateful of hog hooves? All the way home.

A few months later on a morning before I took our kids to school, I printed out a copy of the above story, hoping to proofread it later over a cup of coffee. Once my offspring had been safely deposited, I wheeled into the local convenience store and got my caffeine fix in a paper cup. I went back to my car, settled into the front seat, and picked up the loose manuscript pages I'd brought with me. When I turned to the beginning of the last page, I blinked and read the first lines again: "The whole team was up for the homecoming game. I believe we really played our best. . . ."

Then it hit me. This meant that Zachary had taken his report to school with the last page of my chapter stapled to his homework assignment. His amended report would now read: "The homecoming game was a great disappointment. We all realize that we must overcome our loss if we are to be up for the next game. But I was no longer in a wild and crazy romantic state of mind. . . ."

I threw down the papers, squealed out of the parking lot, and raced to the principal's office where I explained the situation as well as a situation like this can be explained. I might add that Zach's principal, Mr. Stahmer, is a sight to behold. He's at least seven feet tall and just as impressively broad, exactly what seventh through ninth grade boys need in a junior high school administrator. His mere size can be intimidating, even for a *grown-up* who's lost her homework. He was kind—not completely understanding, but kind.

Together we walked up and down halls and searched football fields for signs of Zachary, hoping to catch him before he turned in the fateful paper. Finally, Mr. Stahmer stopped in front of a classroom door and peeked inside.

"He's in here, Mrs. Freeman."

"Oh, good," I replied hopefully, "Maybe we can catch him before he goes to his English class. What class is this?"

"English," he said.

"Ooops," I said.

At that point Mr. Stahmer pushed open the door and asked the teacher if Zachary Freeman had, by any chance, turned in his homework.

Yes, he had. From my position in the hallway outside the door (I had no desire to enter and face my son), I heard the ruffle of papers and the sounds of a teacher chuckling. Soon Zach appeared at the door, red-faced and frantically trying to unstaple my "contribution" to his assignment. He was brief and to the point, though thankfully he is gifted with a sense of humor.

"Mom . . . only you . . . No, don't explain it. Just take it and go home . . . yeah, *now* would be good."

Sometimes I think I was put on this planet to make more messes and embarrassing mistakes than anybody else so that the rest of the world—having met in me the absolute Champion of the Awkward Moment—can press on feeling infinitely better about themselves.

We laugh a lot as a family; it's simply a matter of survival. We've found there are few shortcomings that can't be helped by a healthy dose of humor. And so far—whether it's intentional or not—I'm seeing to it that everyone gets their daily spoonful around here.

A cheerful heart is good medicine.

PROVERBS 17:22

TWO

Peculiarity breeds content

Do you really—I mean *really*—think so?" I asked my husband sincerely.

"Oh, Becky, *everybody* thinks so," Scott stated unequivocally.

So what was the subject of our discussion? It was my husband's opinion—and, according to him, the rest of the world's opinion—that I am a *peculiar* person.

It's not all that bad to be labeled "peculiar," really. Webster defines peculiarity as "something that belongs to only one person, thing, class, people; a distinguishing feature." I rather like that definition. *Unique* has a nicer ring to it, but *peculiar* will do just fine.

One of my most distinguishing features of late is my fingernails. You see—oh how can I explain this? I have none. There. I've admitted it. And I don't mean that they are short or bitten down to the nub. I mean, for the most part, they are nonexistent.

It all started when we went to the Christian Booksellers Convention in Denver, Colorado, last summer. Our publicist told my mother and me to be prepared to sign nearly two hundred copies of our book *Worms in My Tea*. "Wow!" I shouted over the phone, "Do you really think that many people will want to get copies of our book?"

"Oh sure," she answered. "We're giving them away."

Well, even if it was a freebie-give-away deal, the event still fell under the category of a "booksigning." And if my hands would be on display for two hundred bookstore managers, I intended to make memorable encounters. I would begin by having my own nubby nails professionally covered up with the most beautiful fakes I could afford. Thus innocently began a vicious cycle I am still coping with six months later.

From the day I walked into the beauty salon, I should have seen the handwriting on the wall. When the manicurist kept insisting that I relax, stating that I was one of the most tense manicures she'd ever sanded, I should have politely taken my leave. Instead, I courageously squeezed back tears and nodded toward the patch of blood oozing from my index finger directly beneath where Attila the Beautician's file was flying back and forth at warp speed. But I have to admit that as soon as the swelling and bruises subsided (on my fingers, not the manicurist), my new set of acrylic nails indeed looked gorgeous.

By the time I arrived in Denver, I found myself using copious gestures when given the opportunity (yes, even making opportunities) for the sheer pleasure of waving my new nails around. Pointing was a great deal of fun. So was scratching Scott's neck. It wasn't until I was asked to sign an actual book that I realized there was going to be more to owning fingernails of length than I had bargained for. I came at the page, pen in hand, from a variety of angles. However, with my newly extended appendages, I may as well have been writing with a large pogo stick. My signature would not have passed preschool penmanship.

After signing the one hundredth book, I began to experience some success by squeezing the pen tightly between my knuckles. But my fingers eventually grew numb in that position, and I'm afraid it finally began to affect my thinking processes. Originally, my desire had been to come up with catchy individual greetings above my signature like "Wormly Yours," "Love, Laughter, and Joy," or "May you find laughter in all your worms." I preferred that no two messages be exactly alike. After the hundred and fiftieth book, my mind began to wander, and I found myself writing odd salutations from bits of hymns I'd sung in childhood. I vaguely remember signing one book, "All Glory, Laud, and Honor, Becky Freeman." I know the recipient of that copy is still shaking her head wondering exactly what message I was trying to convey. I have no idea, but it was certainly heartfelt.

Scott took this new change in my hands' personality in stride, until one night when he was trying to get to sleep and heard me crunching away on what he assumed was a bag of tortilla chips.

"Becky," he moaned, "cut it out. What are you eating at this time of night anyway?"

"My fake fingernails," I answered matter of factly, "Want a bite?"

I have never had a problem with nail-biting in my entire life. At least not until I acquired the artificial variety. Suddenly nail-biting took on an almost gourmet flavor. I've chewed off acrylic nails, gel nails, and plastic nails. All delicious. The problem is that with each set of nails I bite off, my natural nails also peel off one layer at a time. My real nails now look as though my hands have been through a meat grinder, so I'm forced to cover them up when I go out in public. Now do you understand the vicious cycle I've begun?

To save money on my nail addiction, I've learned to apply them myself. Another benefit of do-it-yourself nails is that I can avoid the bloodletting at the beauty salon. The drawback is the danger inherent in allowing a peculiar person, such as myself, to run around freely armed with a large bottle of Super Nail Glue.

Just the other day, I was trying to glue on a nail while I was driving to a luncheon for professional writers in Dallas. Have to look sharp when we're among professionals, now don't we? To make a long story short, I spilled the glue inside the plastic trash can/drink holder that sits between the front seats of my station wagon. Why I did it I still don't know, but instinctively I crammed my hand into the spilled glue and when I brought it back up, the plastic trash can/drink holder was now a permanent appendage on the end of my arm. I thought to myself, *This simply won't do. Can't very well walk into Steak and Ale with a trash can attached to one's right hand!*

While maneuvering the steering wheel with my knees, I used my one unattached hand to peel off the plastic device. The pain was intense, but I kept myself from screaming aloud by using my old Lamaze childbirth breathing technique. However, when I looked at my hand, I almost let out a screech anyway. Tiny bits of trash—old cookie crumbs and pieces of gum wrapper—were super-glued to my fingers. Luckily, I had a file handy to sand the stuff off, and I sailed into the meeting exuding professionalism.

So you can see why my husband (and a few other people) has come to believe I am peculiar. I have to admit, since becoming a "real author," my life seems to be combing new depths of peculiarity. One moment I feel saucy and intelligent, ready to conquer the world—like Diane Sawyer. The next minute I am unpinning a dry cleaning label from my dress while approaching the podium to speak—suddenly, Minnie Pearl again.

This past year, I have been privileged to meet incredible people, and, at moments, I've even been treated as a near-celebrity. But 98 percent of the time I'm a housewife who lives in a cabin in the boonies with a husband, four kids, two dogs, a bathroom that needs scrubbing, and a frozen chicken that needs thawing. At this moment, I'm typing at my computer wearing hot pink sweatpants, a pink and white striped flannel shirt, a red robe, and socks that don't match. Zach and Zeke, my teenage sons, are watching the television, which is about five feet away from my wall-less "office." Gabriel, our eight-year-old, is wrestling a sleep-over buddy in the back bedroom at top volume. My ten-year-old daughter, Rachel, just walked up, leaned on my shoulder, and informed me that she might throw up any minute now. (She's been home with a virus today.)

Many people think that the circumstances under which I create these chapters might fall under the category of *Peculiar*. (Rachel just returned for more attention, stopping to pinch my upper lip and inform me that I have a mole growing there with a hair sticking out of it. Children certainly know how to keep one humble.)

So even though sophisticated people and agencies occasionally telephone our home/office/school/zoo now—the kind that link their last names with an "&" (i.e., Barnes & Noble, Broadman & Holman, etc.) instead of their first names with an "n" (i.e., Jim Bob 'n' Ida Lou)—I haven't even bothered to change the message on our answering machine to try to make us appear more businesslike. I mean, who do I think I could fool anyway? Executives and neighbors are all greeted by the identical message, delivered with as much Southern hospitality as I can dish out: "Hello, you've reached the home of the Freeman Family and other wildlife." I side with Popeye the Sailorman on this point—"I am what I am."

And what does Scott think of all this? He shakes his head in wonder at what has transpired these past months and pretends he has serious doubts about me and my grandiose adventures—at least in public. But my husband is always the first one I want to see after an exciting bit of news or an interesting encounter or an unusual experience or a new idea. Why? Because, in truth, no one—not one soul on the face of this earth—has shown as much pride and joy at the fact that I am a peculiar woman as has my own husband. He's consistently my best friend and cheerleader, even when my ideas seem hare-brained to everyone else.

Just the other day Scott and I took a walk together down our country road, holding hands. "Becky," he continued on a subject we discuss often, "you are *so* weird. I never met a person in my whole life as strange as you are. But you do intrigue me. When I come home I don't know whether you are going to tell me you've got another book contract, or that you've run over the neighbor's mailbox, or that you tried to sterilize all our tooth-brushes and ended up boiling them into one big plastic glob. I've got to stay around just to see what happens next."

Yes, we've finally accepted the fact that our love is a many-peculiared thing, but it took us awhile to embrace it.

And the LORD hath chosen thee
to be a peculiar people unto himself.

DEUTERONOMY 14:2, KJV

THREE

Cut him some slack so he can go fish!

Would it surprise you to know I was a bride at age seventeen, and Scott, an eighteen-year-old groom? "How on earth did that happen?" you may be asking. Believe it or not, if it had been in frontier days, we might have married even sooner.

When we met in our youth group at church, I was thirteen, Scott was fourteen. It would be two more years before we would be considered boyfriend and girlfriend, but that most intimate of all acts between a man and a woman happened right away—we *talked.*

We were returning home from a trip to Mexico with a bus full of kids from a youth mission trip (probably returning from a lecture warning against getting married too young). It was nighttime and Scott and I converged, sitting on the floor near the rear of the old bus, with hours ahead of us to talk and get acquainted. Because I didn't have big brothers or much experience with boys in general, I always felt awkward making conversation with guys. Not so with Scott. It was effortless. And we didn't discuss weather or sports or school, either. We talked of God and the meaning of life. We shared our ideas about love, our secret hopes and dreams for the future.

Even at age fourteen, Scott had an uncanny way of skipping over preliminaries and getting right to the heart of people. At that moment he became the first real boy I considered a friend. Not a boyfriend, mind you, but a friend who just happened to be male.

It was impossible for me to picture being anything but a buddy to Scott at that point in time. I was too relaxed around him. Too able to be myself. There were no nervous jitters or butterflies, so this couldn't possibly lead to anything romantic, I had reasoned. Even stranger, now that I look back on it, Scott was the best-looking guy at church. His reputation for being the Champion Hayride Kisser was known far and wide—the girls were falling all over themselves to get his attention. I can't believe I didn't join the herd right away, but years later Scott told me he had prayed a prayer that night on the bus.

"Lord, please give me a wife like Becky. And until You do, I'm not going to date another girl." True to his vow, Scott put his lips on hold for The Right Woman. For two years during the ages when most boys go after girls with unprecedented frenzy, Scott patiently bided his time. It eventually paid off.

At the end of those two years, he and I went on another mission trip, this time to Guatemala and El Salvador. By the time we said good-bye to our summer adventure, we were hopelessly in love. And was I ever thrilled to be the recipient of those famous kisses! I still am, but like everybody else who has ever married, or who will ever marry in the future, we had no idea what we were getting into. All the premarital counseling in the world can't prepare us for the reality of sharing life with another person at very close range. I guess it was inevitable that we would make most of the mistakes it is possible to make. One of the first had to do with getting tangled up in a fishing line—The Invisible Marriage Fishing Line.

You haven't heard of it? Well, then I'm going to let you in on a little secret: When couples get married they are tied together by an invisible fishing line. From that moment on, their goal is to keep the line pulled just so—not giving it too much slack but not pulling it too taut, either. When there is excessive slack, the two of them get all tangled up and in each other's way constantly. The fancy term psychologists use for such situations is *becoming enmeshed*. On the other hand, when the line is pulled too taut, the husband and wife become so independent that the line can easily break under the strain—and there's nothing left binding them together anymore. The professional word for this stage is *polarization*—where one partner is basically running toward the North Pole while the other flies due South.

Keeping the tension in the line in balance requires paying attention and constantly checking the drag. If a couple becomes fairly adept at keeping the fishing line just right, they may actually hit the stage of Balanced Relational Health termed *interdependence*. I wish someone had explained this invisible fishing line to me during premarital counseling. Maybe they did, and our ears were stopped up with youthful infatuation.

Just two months after I turned seventeen, I graduated early from high school, married Scott, and went straight from my parent's home to my husband's duplex. So I never had an opportunity to be a woman of independence. If there is one thing I regret about marrying at age seventeen, it is that I never experienced college dorms, or having my own apartment, or having a time in my life that I could look back on and call my own. I have no "single days" on which to reminisce. I went directly from being someone's daughter to being someone's wife. As a result, I clung to Scott, wanting him to fulfill all my identity needs—and nearly choked him to death in the process.

If, for example, Scott were five minutes late coming home from work and I happened to hear a siren in the distance, I would be sobbing at a neighbor's door in an instant—convinced my young husband had been fatally injured on his motorcycle.

When he did come through the door, I was so overjoyed to see him upright and breathing that I would often run and jump into his arms, wrapping my legs around his waist and nearly knocking the breath out of him like an overly enthusiastic golden retriever.

To Scott, my arms around his neck probably began to feel more like vise grips. Fortunately, with the passage of time, my fears eased. Within five years we also had two young sons to help occupy my overactive imagination. But there was one pivotal experience we still refer to as "The Time Becky Decided, Once and for All, to Give Scott Some Slack."

The saga began one summer afternoon when Scott came home from a hot day of roofing and announced that he and his partner were going to take off for a little rest and relaxation. They planned to ride their motorcycles to Arkansas to do some trout fishing.

All I could visualize at that moment was Scott's body lying mangled on a highway or floating facedown in some mountain stream. I put my twenty-two-year-old foot down. I would not allow it, I said. He said he did not need my permission, nor had he asked for it. For three days I cried and begged him not to go, but he would not be moved. The morning he walked out the door and resolutely mounted his motorcycle, I sat down cross-legged on the shag carpet in our living room, holding a baby and a toddler close to my chest, and sobbed as if their father had already been pronounced dead.

Somehow I managed to survive the rest of the day. But I distinctly remember eating at Taco Muncho and looking wistfully out the big picture window, over the top of a burrito and my babies' heads. Just then a young guy on a motorcycle drove into view, and waves of grief hit me again. I gathered up the kids and barely made it out the door and into the car before I collapsed into tears again.

Finally, it dawned on me that I could not spend the next 120 hours bawling. My eyes had swelled nearly shut and I was making the kids miserable. I would have to do something constructive to take my mind off Scott's lifeless body on the highway and streams of Arkansas.

So I planned some outings. I had a couple of friends and their wee ones over for lunch. By the fourth day of Scott's absence, I was beginning to have a pretty good time. Then I went to visit my parents at their home across town. As I was sitting at their kitchen table munching on chips and laughing at something cute little Zachary had just said, Mother suggested the kids and I drive with them to Sweetwater to see my grandmother, Nonnie. It was starting to sound fun, and I was grateful for another diversion. Then the phone rang. It was Scott.

He was having a terrific time. However, unbeknownst to me, he was suffering from a belated guilt trip. So he offered a plan he thought would ease his conscience and make me happy at the same time.

"Hey, Becky," he said on the other end of the line, "I've got a great idea. How about you pack up the boys and take a bus up here and join us? It's really pretty country."

In my mind, I was thinking, *Gee, I'm just about to adjust to the idea of being a single mom for a week. Actually, I'm even starting to have fun. I was looking forward to going to Sweetwater too. But Scott must be missing us terribly to ask me to take such a long bus trip, with a two-year-old and a baby, to meet him. Poor, lonely thing! How could I possibly turn him down in his hour of need?*

In the space of a few hours I was boarding a bus with a baby on each hip. But with each turn of the giant wheels and every fresh whiff of diesel fuel, I knew I'd made a terrible mistake. If Baby Zeke wasn't wet or dirty or crying or nursing, Toddler Zachary was spitting or biting or whining. Seventeen agonizing and sleepless hours later, we dismounted into a tiny, filthy bus station somewhere in the hills of Arkansas. It was four o'clock in the morning. Now I was spitting, biting, and whining.

When Scott and his buddy, Randy, showed up at the station, we were faced with a dilemma. How would we drive from the station to the cabin? Motorcycles were our only form of affordable, available transportation. I know it was soooooo stupid and soooooo dangerous and I could still kick myself for it, but all of us ended up riding to the camp on Scott's motorcycle. By zipping Baby Zeke in Scott's leather jacket and placing little Zachary between Scott's back and my stomach, we could all fit on one Honda. I was suddenly a motorcycle mama in every sense of the word, but I was far from proud of the fact.

When we arrived at the cabin, there was more cause for concern. First of all, the cabin consisted of one big room with two beds, a kitchenette in the corner, and a bathroom—it would have to house me, Scott, our two boys, and Randy. When I checked the small refrigerator, it contained nothing but a cool box of worms and a few canned drinks. And there was precious little money left in the food budget after Scott paid for my luxurious bus trip. I could tell right off the bat it was going to be a real challenge for me to be a happy camper.

While the guys went trout fishing, I walked across the dirt road to a questionable looking Bait & Beer shop carrying the baby in my backpack and holding my toddler by the hand. There I purchased a loaf of bread, two dozen eggs, butter, and milk. For breakfast we had French toast, for lunch we had toast and eggs, and for dinner I served fried egg sandwiches. The same menu was duplicated the next day, only I reversed the order for variety.

But it wasn't until night fell that the real nightmare began. It was awkward enough to be sleeping in the same room with Scott's business partner, but I could deal with that. The worst part was that Randy snored. And from his bunk only five feet away from us, I could tell immediately that this was not just your average snore. Oh, no. Randy had a snore to be reckoned with—it would have registered at least a 7.5 on the Richter scale.

I woke Scott a couple of times and begged him to go over to Randy's bed and give him a good hard shake. He finally did, and there was blessed relief for all of ten seconds. Then with the force of a seagoing foghorn, Randy's sinuses geared up again—this time with a vengeance. I got out of my bed, took my pillow and blanket into the bathroom, and stuffed my ears with torn-up pieces of toilet tissue. The foghorn continued to blare, even through the closed door and with water running in the sink. I finally cried myself to sleep in an empty bathtub with towels and pillows stacked over my head.

After a few days of this "blissful" vacation, Scott wearily helped me and the kids board the big bus toward home. The seventeen-hour trip back home gave me plenty of time to ponder the absurdity of this situation. When the trauma finally came to an end, and all of us made it safely back home, I kissed my shag carpeting. I had learned my lesson and was more than ready to let go some slack on the Marriage Fishing Line.

Since then, I've made a concerted attempt to look happy—almost gleeful—when Scott goes off on one of his "guy trips." The last thing I want to do is make him feel bad about getting away for a little free time. I simply don't have the strength to pay for any more guilt trips.

Scott, on the other hand, never seemed to struggle as much with giving me space. For the most part, he has always been delighted to let me spread my wings and try new experiences. Besides, when I'm gone it gives him and the kids a chance to bond—and eat pizza in the living room without getting yelled at.

I remember returning home last spring after attending a three-day writers conference. I walked into the living room, expecting to be greeted by hugs and kisses and choruses of "We missed you!" Instead, Scott and the kids sat entranced by some television show. I cleared my throat and began telling them how I was going to be speaking in front of important people soon and how impressed they should be to claim me as their wife and mother.

No one batted an eyelash. Just yak, yak, yak about a football game or something.

"But don't worry," I continued my soliloquy, "even with fame and fortune knocking at my door I'll always keep you, Dear Family, first in my heart."

"That's nice, Dear," Scott commented as he wrestled Zachary for the remote control. Seeing such callous disregard in the presence of greatness, I could contain myself no longer. Walking directly through the mass of tangled bodies on the living room floor, I positioned myself in front of the television.

"I AM QUEEN!" I announced at the top of my lungs.

From Scott's horizontal position on the floor he hollered in my general direction, "Hey, Your Highness, get me a Dr. Pepper, will you?" The fishing line pulled me to earth with a jerk. (However, be assured Scott got his own Dr. Pepper.)

Isn't that the way it always goes? Married people are constantly playing at this game of marital checks and balances, of adjusting the drag on each other's lines. And couples seem to be constantly shifting roles to help balance out the other.

One may say, "Here—have some free time—grow and stretch—enjoy!"

But then he senses something has gone too far, so he adjusts the drag and pulls in some of the slack. "Hey—wait a minute, you're getting too far away."

Then, perhaps, he realizes he jerked the line *too* hard and hurt feelings in the process. Another adjustment is needed. "Oh, I'm sorry. I didn't mean to *burst* your balloon—just *deflate* it a little. Let me give you a hug. I *am* really proud of your accomplishment."

In time, more tugging is felt on the line and he responds enthusiastically but with a gentle warning. "Need some more space, you say? Go for it—fly away for a new adventure! But don't forget where your home and heart are, OK?"

Mother says that being married is like taking on a Siamese twin for life. In most things we do, that other person has to be considered. Marriage is often the school to which God sends us in order to learn what it means to be less than totally centered in ourselves—to begin to give consideration to the needs and desires of another, and then in widening circles, many others. But at the same time, we need time alone—to pursue our own dreams or to get together with our own friends.

And so it goes. Push and pull. "Let me go!" "Wait—hold me close!" The line stretches and loosens in a perpetual dance of adjustment. Once in awhile, between "too taut" and "too much slack," we experience brief moments of Balanced Relational Health. Most of the time, however, we're busy flopping around in stages of Unbalanced Relational Lopsidedness. Still, I prefer to deal with tangles and stretched-out lines than to live a life of total autonomy. I understand that autonomy is very poor company on a cold night.

He said, "Let me go . . . . If I have found favor in your eyes, let me get away to see my brothers."

1 Samuel 20:29

FOUR

Showdown at the hoedown

Under normal circumstances my husband can gracefully tolerate any number of my faults. I can back over multiple mailboxes, get stuck in ditches, leave my purse in out-of-town restaurants, and forget to mail important checks, yet all is quickly forgiven.

But in our earlier married life there was one thing my husband had never been able to tolerate, not even for a second, and that was for me to be in a negative mood. His attitude was, "Get over it and get over it yesterday." Here was an area in our marriage where I had come to feel *I* wasn't being given any slack in the ol' fishing line—no leeway to express even one moment of plain old everyday grumpiness. Once every month we added my drop in hormones to Scott's lack of tolerance, and we had an explosion just waiting to happen. Unfortunately, one time happened to coincide with my birthday.

Scott and I were driving to Dallas to meet my parents at a country-western family steak house, The Trail Dust, to celebrate. The Trail Dust had long been a family favorite; it had a wonderful band and was one of the few wholesome places where we could go to two-step, waltz, or Cotton-Eyed-Joe. Mother and Daddy were getting to be quite the fancy country-western dancers and we had always enjoyed each others' company, so we were looking forward to the evening out with them.

As we were driving, I mulled over the variety of special occasions we'd celebrated at this ranch house over the years—Scott's graduation from college, numerous birthdays, and a couple of anniversaries. Then, however, I recalled a couple of special celebrations that had been a little hard on my ego. On my thirtieth birthday, for example, the band leader had coerced me into coming up to the front, donning a white cowboy hat, and galloping around the dance floor on a stick horse while the packed-out restaurant sang "Happy Birthday to You." Now, isn't that special? I'd been stuck in one of those classic unavoidable dilemmas. If I declined to trot around the floor like an overgrown child on a stick horse, I would have looked like a spoilsport. If I accepted the invitation, I would look like an idiot. Better to be an Idiot than a Party Pooper, so I pranced proudly with my head held high and my dignity still somewhat intact.

But there had been yet another celebration dinner at the Trail Dust I remembered that had pretty much stripped me of any remaining vestiges of pride. That evening, Scott and I had been seated across the table from some rather dignified young men from our church—one was an engineer, the other a physician. To this day I don't know how it happened because I had certainly not been drinking anything stronger than root beer, but as I was debating a serious point, I became airborne and somehow fell straight back in my chair and onto the floor. There I sat in my ladder-back chair, staring at the *ceiling* instead of across the table at the two young men.

Of course, I was wearing a dress. Of course, I landed with my boots sticking straight up in the air. As nonchalantly as he might have reached for a fallen set of keys, Scott scooped me up and, without a word, set me back in the upright position. Didn't lose a beat. Just propped me up like a rag doll and went right on with his meal and conversation. The two gentlemen, as I recall, sat poised with forks in midair, blinking as if to be sure of what they had just seen.

As we drove toward my birthday celebration, I recalled these past events and felt suddenly uneasy about another Trail Dust celebration. As Scott and I neared the halfway point on the highway to the familiar steak house, my general uneasiness turned to strong irritation coupled with a sudden high-dosage bolt of low self-esteem, and things went downhill from there.

"So why don't you like my dress, Scott?" I began.

"I didn't say I didn't like your dress!"

"Well, you didn't say you *did*, either. And you didn't say I looked pretty tonight. You always tell me I look ravishing when we go out. What is it? Do I look heavy? Are you embarrassed to have me as your partner?"

"I'm not going to have this conversation, Becky."

"You are talking to me, so you *are* having this conversation."

Silence followed for the next thirty minutes. I guessed maybe we *weren't* having this conversation after all. When we pulled into the restaurant parking lot, I could stand it no longer.

"I can't believe you ruined my birthday dinner by refusing to tell me I look ravishing!"

Then I flounced out of the truck, slammed the door hard enough to loosen every tooth in his head, and marched into the steak house. I was pretty sure Scott would follow me, even though my behavior was not all that ravishing. After all, it was my birthday and we were meeting my parents, for goodness sake. But did I mention that my husband has a wee stubborn streak?

I walked into the restaurant and glanced back over my shoulder, expecting to see a properly penitent husband. There was a huge empty space instead. So I made up a plausible excuse to tell my parents. I told them that Scott had probably gone to get some gas and would be right back, all the while inwardly hoping that what I said would turn out to be the truth. I kept a sharp eye peeled for him—even praying that he would walk through those swinging doors any minute and the standoff would be over. But no sign of my tall husband graced the entry. After about twenty minutes I ran out of excuses. We were into a standoff to rival the one at the O.K. Corral. But no longer up to a shoot-out, I began to cry into my iced tea.

Not knowing what else to do, Daddy asked me if I would like to dance, and I managed to nod. So I "Waltzed Across Texas" in my father's arms while the tears poured down my cheeks over the fact that my birthday dinner had been ruined, my husband was behaving like a stubborn mule sitting out in the parking lot, and, most of all, I was not ravishing tonight.

Finally, I told my parents that Scott and I had had a little tiff on the way to the restaurant. They both managed to feign surprise and registered the appropriate sympathy for me. Then I told them that if they would excuse me I had to go out to the parking lot to apologize to my hard-headed, insensitive husband.

I found Scott sitting in the truck, his hard head resting against the steering wheel. As soon as I opened the door, Scott took a good look at my tear-stained face. "Becky," he said grimly, "what time of the month is it?"

How *like* a man—so totally irrational!

"It's my birthday. That's what time of the month it is. Did you know that it is my *birthday?* How can you stand me up on my *birthday?* And in front of my *parents!*"

"Becky, I'm sorry," he said, shaking his head as if to clear it. "I just don't know what to *do* with you. You're like a different person when you hit a certain time of the month. You hate yourself. And you try your best to pick a fight with me. And it works every time! You've got to do *something!*"

I felt tremendous relief that he wasn't going to leave me stranded there and began to hope the evening could be salvaged.

I even toyed with the remote possibility he might be a tiny bit right.

"Well," I said, sniffing and trying to smile, "I'll make you a deal. I'll see a doctor soon if you'll come inside and do the Cotton-Eyed-Joe with me."

When we walked back inside the restaurant and to our table arm in arm, Mother shook her head and grinned.

"You know, you two are a lot of trouble—but you're never more trouble than you're worth. Let's eat!"

We made it through the evening, even managed to have a good time. Once as I waltzed in my husband's arms, he stopped and whispered something in my ear that I desperately needed to hear.

"Miss Becky, you look ravishing tonight."

The end of a matter is better than its beginning,
and patience is better than pride.

ECCLESIASTES 7:8

FIVE

Hot-blooded heartthrobs on slow boil

I wish I could say that that one waltz fixed everything that was haywire in our marriage. But the truth is, the showdowns kept coming with alarming regularity.

I've often compared Scott and myself to a hot-blooded Italian couple. Now, I *look* the part. Italian or Spanish either one, they're both supposed to be hot-blooded, aren't they? I look like the type you might expect to find dancing on a table in a cantina with a pair of castanets clicking.

Scott, on the other hand, looks like the all-American guy—tall, lanky but broad shouldered, wheat-colored hair, square jawed. The kind of good-looking guy that could make a woman salivate, present company included.

Who knows what made us spark with so much anger? I guess it's the same thing that made us passionate about each other when things were good. We're just two very *intense* people. Plus, we *were* teenagers when we married, and in many ways, I think we got locked into a pattern of relating to each other like a couple of kids.

Scott and I were good, well-mannered children. We were each considered easy-going and agreeable. Maybe we were just saving up our tempers all those years for the day we could get married and go berserk.

So what, exactly, had we two "crazy kids" been arguing about all this time? Probably the same things every couple fights about. Perhaps our conflicts *were* a bit more—shall we say—theatrical, but the subject matter is fairly universal.

After having been married for three years, we began the classic struggle of starting a family. Baby Arrives. Man Watches Lover Turn into Mother. Man Misses Wife. Woman Feels Pulled in Two. Baby Drains Available Energy Needed for Couple to Do Anything about It. Just when Life Gets under Control, the Home Pregnancy Test Turns Blue Again.

Then we fought about how to raise the little tykes—how to discipline, how old they should be before being punished, and when discipline should be administered. How much attention they should have, how long they should be allowed to cry at bedtime, and how much our lives should revolve around them.

Every now and again when Scott and I see a young couple with babies and toddlers, we each have the overpowering urge to cry. We so empathize with that difficult, wonderful, exhausting, precious, draining time of life. As our kids have grown older, these conflicts have abated, but the Preschool Decade certainly took its toll.

We have each been jealous of the other's work, the kids, attractive coworkers of the opposite sex, *un*attractive coworkers of the opposite sex, time-demanding projects, good causes, television, engrossing books, church activities, best friends, rutabagas—well, maybe not rutabagas. Whatever was perceived as having more value in the eyes of our mate than ourselves left us open for feeling neglected. Our insecurities screamed, "Pay attention to me!"

We fought often over finances: bouncing the checking account; scraping the bottom of the piggy bank for kids' lunch money; bouncing the checking account; having to ask the chief wage earner for money (which always leaves the "askee" feeling like a needy child); bouncing the checking account; having to "sweat it out" over bills, needs for our children, grocery money, doctor appointments, and the ability to keep our thoroughly used cars on the road; bouncing the checking account; wondering if it is better for a mother to work and help out with financial tension or to scrimp by so she can stay home with kids; and finally, in case I haven't mentioned it yet, bouncing the checking account.

Even now, on Paying Bills Night when Scott sinks into a chair with envelopes waiting to be stuffed with money we don't have, a dark, ominous cloud settles over the entire house. Instinctively, the kids and I begin walking on tiptoe. We find ourselves gently touching each other on the shoulder as we pass in the hall like survivors of some past crises. Sometimes we whisper soothing words of comfort to each other: "It's almost over now. Daddy's nose isn't flaring as wide as it was a few minutes ago."

We both have struggled with periods of low self-esteem. Here's an example of a typical anger-producing conversation when the female of a relationship is suffering from a drop in self-confidence.

"Honey," she begins, "am I getting too fat, or do you think these jeans are shrinking?"

"The jeans look the same size to me."

"Then find some other skinny girl to squeeze into them. There's no way I'm going out looking like a giant rump roast tonight!"

And here's a conversation where the male of our species is experiencing a period of diminished self-esteem. Notice the man exhibiting the male tendency to lean toward defensiveness.

"How was your day, Sweetheart?" he begins.

"Oh, fine. I bought groceries, fed the kids, and the house is clean. I *am* a little tired though. I'm looking forward to a good night's rest."

"Oh, sure. Why don't you just *save* the big rejection speech and say, 'Not tonight, Dear!'"

Do any of these scenarios sound familiar? The only common cause of discord we haven't experienced is "a lack of communication." We may be communicating in loud, obnoxious, staccato voices, but we are rarely at a loss for words. Our love is intense. Our anger is intense. Our communication is intense. We are just your plain old everyday, average, amazingly intense couple. And that is why we were ready to call it quits one day, and the next morning we were committed to live together in passionate union for all eternity. Understand? No? Well, you're in good company. Neither do we. It just is.

But if there gets to be *too* many conflicts—no matter what the source—it is easy to wake up one day and find oneself in the danger zone. I had no idea how close we were.

What causes fights and quarrels among you? Don't they come from your desires that battle within you? You want something but don't get it.

JAMES 4:1–2

SIX

If I hear that song again, I'll scream!

I couldn't breathe. I couldn't think. The world was tilted on edge and sliding into blackness. Somehow I made my way through the haze of chattering children in the school cafeteria and into the teacher's lounge. There, my red-rimmed eyes met those of Laticia's, a fellow teacher. She immediately understood my need for help and put her arm around my shoulders. She carefully led me to an empty hall where I collapsed in sobs.

Laticia is a tiny woman with beautiful, creamy, coffee-colored skin, and she has a fiery strength about her. Right now, I needed her strength. I had none left of my own.

"What is it, Becky?" she gently asked when my tears began to subside. "What's the matter?"

"Oh, Laticia, it's over. My marriage is over! I just talked to Scott on the phone, and he sounded so cold, so distant. He said he's made his decision. He can't stand to watch us hurt each other any more. He wants a divorce, and he says there's nothing I can do to change his mind."

Usually talkative, Laticia was quiet, letting me pour out my pain.

"He's right, you know," I continued. "Our relationship has been one exhausting experience after another. It's up and down and back and forth. One moment we're at each other's throats, the next we're madly in love. But after these last few months we're like pieces of elastic that have been stretched one too many times. We're worn out. We just don't have it in us to keep bouncing back. It's like walking around nitroglycerin, never knowing what might set off the next explosion. Is this any way to live? Oh, God, what am I going to do? How will we tell our children? Is this really going to happen to *us?*"

I felt as though my chest had been ripped open and my heart pulled out. It physically ached. I had never felt such a relentless wrenching. *Lord, I can't take this pain.* Then I remembered my class. I had to go and get my twenty first-graders from the playground, take them back to my room, and teach them math. *How can I have a nervous breakdown in the middle of a school day? In five more minutes I have to add two-digit numbers together in front of a class of seven-year-olds. I have to calm down. Good teachers don't fall apart in front of the children. We're professionals. But today, oh dear God, I'm a child.*

Laticia was one step ahead of me.

"Listen to me, Becky. Get your kids, and then bring them into my classroom. They can watch a movie with my class this afternoon. You take what time you need to pull yourself together. Then we need to talk."

My first-graders and I knew each other well at this point in the year. I loved them, and they loved me back, as children are so easily prone to do. After bringing them in from recess, I led the little guys and gals back to my classroom. Then I sat down on my reading stool, tissue in hand, and managed, between sniffs, to talk to them.

"Kids, you know how some days you have to come to school—but you are hurting inside because you've had a disagreement with Mom or Dad that morning?" They all nodded in sympathy. "Sometimes you even cry. Well, Mrs. Freeman is having some of those hurt feelings, and I need you to be especially kind today. In a minute I'm going to take you to the class next door and let you watch a movie so I can take a few minutes to rest and feel better."

As they filed out the door one by one, each of my students said, "We love you, Mrs. Freeman" or "I hope you feel better." Children's arms reached out to pat and hug, to comfort the "professional." Their open tenderness helped.

I dropped off the children at Laticia's door, thanking this mentor-teacher for her kindness. As I walked away, I thought, *She's a good friend, but she can't possibly understand any of this. I see the way she and her husband love each other. The way he picks her up at 4:00 sharp on Wednesdays for their "date night." The flowers he sends, the beautiful clothes he buys for her. Weekend get-a-ways. The romantic ways they talk about one another. If only . . .* but it was useless to waste wishes on what could never be.

I went back to my empty classroom, turned out the lights, lay my head on my desk, and wept again. It seemed the tears would never stop, and like one of my first-graders, I wondered where bodies store all that salt water. My mind drifted over the years with Scott. I loved him. I knew he loved me. How, then, had it come to this?

We'd had the most romantic of courtships. We'd never had a single disagreement; we were Romeo and Juliet, lovers for all time and eternity. Sure, we had been just seventeen and eighteen years old when we got married, but we came from good families. We were involved in a solid church and had received the blessing and emotional support of friends and family. And we were both mature for our ages. Everybody said so.

However, not long after the honeymoon we began to realize, with a sense of impending doom, that we were actually living with someone other than the person we had signed up to marry. In spite of the feeling that there had been some mix-up, we still loved each other—maybe even too intensely. Perhaps it was that desperate desire we both had to love and be loved that seemed to increase the intensity of the pain we experienced when we went through periods of disillusionment and perceived rejection. In recent months, those feelings of rejection and anger had almost drowned out all feelings of love.

After years of clumsily walking on eggshells, it was time to face the facts. Our marriage was turning us into scrambled omelets. Divorce, the unthinkable, had gradually become the object of our daydreams. Logic told us that throwing in the towel might cover up some of the mess we were making of each other's lives.

How else could we end the vicious cycle? For seventeen years we seemed doomed to play the same old groove in the same old record. It had sounded like a bad country song, hummed slow and sad, with a "poor me" twang. I could write the lyrics myself.

I start talkin' and a bawlin'
He packs his bags and starts a walkin'
While I'm cryin' in my tea cup
He's sleepin' in the pickup.
Three nights of bein' alone
We miss each other to the bone,
We've got the headache, heartache,
This-is-all-that-I-can-take blues.
Finally tired of feeling smug
Someone reaches for a hug.
Passion lingers for a while
But there's fear behind the smile,
'Cause the song's about to end
Another battle's 'round the bend.
We've got the headache, heartache,
This-is-all-that-I-can-take blues.

And so now it had come to this. Anything—*anything*—but continue to play that same record.

I heard the door open and Laticia entered the room, interrupting my tears and my thoughts. She sat down and looked at me seriously with her big, black eyes before she measured her words carefully.

"Becky, think hard before you give up on your marriage. You've got to fight for your relationship. Charles and I have survived much worse than you and Scott."

It was a startling challenge, one I hadn't expected. My eyes flew open.

"What? But . . . but . . . you and Charles are so . . . together!"

"It hasn't always been that way. We've hurt each other terribly."

I could tell by the intensity in her voice that she meant *horribly* terribly. A faint glimmer of hope lit the dark corners of my mind.

"What did you do?" I asked, dabbing at the edges of my eyes.

"First, we got some counseling. We still go to group sessions. You and Scott probably need outside help. It's like you've both been involved in a bad wreck. When it is this bad, it's time to call an ambulance—a paramedic. Neither of you has the strength to help the other right now. Get help. I promise you, there is such a thing as starting over. But you've got to fight for it."

Fight? I felt whipped already—bone weary. I'd think about her words later. I was just too tired to make important decisions right now.

That evening, I dragged myself through the door of our home, completely drained. Scott would not be coming home tonight, and I didn't really want him to, not the way things were. I preferred to have a quiet supper with the kids and go to bed early, and alone, rather than face another battle. But in another way, I did miss him. I missed the times when we had managed to dodge the minefield and, between battles, had found each other's warm embrace. If only, if *only* . . .

After I put the children to bed, I lay staring into the darkness. I thought of how Scott and I were each capable of being two different people. I felt lonely for a *part* of who Scott was, but not for the other part of him—the part I'd talked to on the phone today. I could manage without that robot-like stranger.

I finally fell asleep with that odd mixture of emotions playing in my head. I dreamed of talking with the Scott who was my old friend about this awful, impossible situation with Scott, my husband who wanted out of our marriage. He had been my best friend since I was fifteen years old. We'd grown up together. Who would I talk to now about this hole that had been left in my heart? I wanted my sixteen-year-old-friend-Scott to magically appear and help me cope with losing my thirty-three-year-old-husband-Scott.

I slept fitfully and woke after the dream. Lying there, I thought of Zachary, Ezekiel, Rachel Praise, and Gabriel. I knew my husband would be thinking of our children tonight too. He loved them so and was a wonderful father. It would be killing him, as it was me now, to think that our own pain would harm their innocent lives. I wondered also, if my husband was lying awake somewhere in the darkness out there missing the "kinder, gentler" part of me.

And though I didn't feel it then, I know it now. There was a Shepherd moving in the blackness, guiding our paths, and keeping watch in our darkest night.

"I will care for My sheep
and will deliver them from all the places
to which they were scattered on a cloudy and gloomy day."

EZEKIEL 34:12, NASB

SEVEN

Does "as long as you both shall live" mean a lifetime guarantee?

The digital clock bleeped 6:00 A.M. The state of our marriage reminded me of the state of Alaska—expansive and cold. Especially when I contemplated the large empty spot beside my pillow that morning.

Like an earthquake victim, I longed to be able to trust solid ground—all those foundations on which I had always been able to depend. But the terra was no longer firma. If my marriage was failing, what about everything else I believed in? *Does God care about us? Is He even out there at all?* It was as if the tidy box containing all I had known and believed was shaken of its contents. And what, if anything, would I be able to put back into my box of beliefs?

I've since learned that having your box tipped over is always frightening, but it usually happens to everyone at some time. Often it is the only way to clean out the junk, making way for fresh beginnings. Eventually what goes back into the box is yours and yours alone. No hand-me-down belief systems or other people's treasures.

Rolling over toward the nightstand, I flipped on the radio—hungry for the sound of a human voice, even if it had to come from a small, black box. The "Let's Get Up and at 'Em" hosts were talking about the weather forecast and arguing about some obscure bill floating around in Congress. Then, with total disregard for my personal crisis, the perky morning DJs began cracking perky morning jokes.

Didn't everyone know that life as we'd known it had come to a complete halt? I thought to myself, *A newscaster—a Walter Cronkite-type—should be breaking in any minute now to announce, "This bulletin just in: Scott and Becky Freeman, adorable couple and parents of four remarkable children, are on the verge of marital collapse! A National State of Emergency has officially been declared."*

Instead, those Good Morning morons were droning on about cumulous cloud formations as if nothing else of significance had happened yesterday! Incredible! As I wondered how the rest of society could continue their trivial little lives in the midst of Our Relationship Trauma, I could almost hear Scott's voice, teasing me: "Just because you've always been able to charm the hair off a bullfrog, you assume the world revolves around *you*, Darlin'. Someday you might be in for a surprise."

Well, as Gomer Pyle used to say, "Sur-PRISE, sur-PRISE, sur-PRISE." *Someday* had arrived with a bang. It was painfully obvious the world didn't take its daily spin with me as its permanent axis.

So here I was, in the middle of the worst personal crisis of my life, the sun still rising routinely in my eastern window. The numbers on the clock still clicking ever onward. Radio personalities still trying to get laughs before 10:00 A.M. Even under the best of circumstances—in peacetime—I've always thought it was in bad taste for people to try to be amusing in the morning.

In desperate need of comfort, I shut off the radio and reached for the Bible on the nightstand. At that point, I knew my situation warranted using the most theologically advanced method of gleaning insight from the Word of God. So I closed my eyes, opened my Bible, and randomly stuck my finger on a verse. Honestly, I was too hurt and confused for a system that might have required more effort.

It always amazes me that God graciously chooses to meet me at my point of need, however pitiful my efforts to reach Him. The Shepherd comes after His lost, disoriented sheep when He hears their bleating, no matter how faint or weak their cries.

As my stomach turned in knots over whether or not my husband would—or should—come home, my eyes rested on Proverbs 27:8: "Like a bird that wanders from her nest, so is a man who wanders from his home" (NASB).

At that instant the churning in my belly stopped. The Good Shepherd was clearly showing me that my husband, no matter what he said in anger and frustration, had wandered from his nest. Furthermore, as a bird longs to get back to her young, my husband, at this very moment, was missing his home—his family. Even, perhaps, *me*. My prayerful response to that deep revelation was, "Dear Lord, Scott is feeling just as lost and alone and miserable as I am. Oh, *good!*"

Since the world had not blown up, I still had to get dressed and ready for work. My four children also had to be prodded, breakfasted, and delivered to the bus stop. Somehow, I struggled through the next two days. Other than letting me know where he'd be staying, there was no other communication. During those days, I stumbled from being courageous, positive, and self-assured; to angry, resentful, and fed up; to blubbering like a vulnerable little girl. On the second day of Scott's absence as I was driving home from teaching school, I thought again of what Laticia had said earlier.

"You and Scott will have to fight for your marriage. It's hard, especially at first. But you have to decide if your love is worth the effort."

I cried again—half talking to myself, half in prayer. "*Is* it worth it, Lord? Wouldn't it be better to bow out gracefully now, rather than risk doing any more damage?"

Not wanting to think, I reached for the radio dial and turned it on. A song by Michael Martin Murphy filled the air. I'd always loved the melody, but this time the words held even greater impact.

"Right in their hands is a dying romance
and they're not even trying to keep it alive.

What's the glory of living?
Doesn't anybody ever stay together anymore?
And if nothing ever lasts forever—tell me,
What's forever for?"[1]

The words struck like an arrow in the core of my heart. Forever. I always thought true love would last forever. My mind drifted back to an altar, a seventeen-year-old girl draped in white lace, an eighteen-year-old boy decked out in a white tuxedo with tails—and a vow.

But, we were just babies. We didn't really know what we were saying! I continued to argue with myself.

Yes, Becky, you didn't know all the pain marriage would entail. But you were fully aware of the promise you were making to that young man before family, friends, and God Almighty. You knew forever meant a fair amount of time. It was a promise you really intended to keep. A vow!

I had no rebuttal for that round. As a matter of fact, I could remember exactly what I had said to my bridegroom on June 27, 1976, because I'd composed the words myself: *"Scott, I promise to be your faithful wife until one of us lays the other in the waiting arms of the Savior or until we meet Him in the air together."*

People always said I had a way with words. And I'd certainly left no room for misunderstanding with *those vows,* had I? No "if" or "but" clauses. Not a loophole—other than Rapture or death—in sight.

Standing there, on the brink of the Canyon of Divorce, reality dawned. Aside from the fact that we had promised, of our own free will, to be faithful to one another, I also began to think of the practical implications of an honest-to-goodness divorce. I thought of the loneliness, of starting over, of dreams dashed, financial stresses, our families torn apart, friends hurt, but most of all, our children caught between the two parents they loved.

Scott and I were living through the "for worse" part of the marriage deal. But what reason for separating could we offer our children that would make any sense? And what sort of lesson would we be teaching them about how to handle problems that would come up in their future relationships? They knew things were tense between their daddy and me, but at the time they had no idea that Scott's absence was more than a business trip. Oh, how I wanted to keep from hurting them!

We can't give up. Not yet. If for nothing else than for the sake of Zachary, Ezekiel, Rachel, and Gabriel.

I twisted the simple gold band around my finger. Those of you who have read our "falling in love" story from *Worms in My Tea and Other Mixed Blessings* may remember the significance of my wedding band. Scott had originally given it to me while we were on a mission trip to Guatemala as a gesture of friendship and budding love. He was sixteen years old at the time; I was fifteen. He'd used the last of his money—twelve dollars—to buy the tiny, rose gold ring. I knew, even then, that if I ever married this guy, the twelve-dollar ring would be the only wedding band I would ever want. I took it off and looked inside at the Scripture reference, Jeremiah 24:6–7—a verse I'd claimed for myself and for Scott at the beginning of our dating relationship.

Maybe there's hope. God keeps His promises much better than we do.

The phone rang, breaking my contemplation. It was Scott, his voice soft and tired. He wanted to take the kids out to dinner.

Said he missed them. Swallowing hard, I asked, "So, how are you feeling about their mother these days?"

"I don't know. I guess I'm just tired of hurting her. Becky, I just want to set you free to find somebody who'll make you happy. I don't know if I can be the kind of guy you need. I'm not a Joe Have-It-All-Together Christian in a three-piece suit."

"If I'd wanted Joe Christian in a three-piece suit, I would have married him. You're the only man I've ever wanted, Scott."

"I can be ornery, and I'll probably always be a sort of rebel."

"I can be frustrating, and I'll probably always be something of a basket case."

"No wonder we've made such a happy couple."

"Oh, Scott. What are we going to do with us?"

"I just don't know if I have it in me to take another run at it, Becky."

"I know. I know. But I've checked the Official Marriage Rules, and they don't seem to allow for throwing in the towel."

"Yeah, but we've broken so many Marriage Rules that I don't know whether there are too many of them left to worry about."

"So you're saying you want to give up?"

"No, I don't want to give up. Everything I've loved and worked for is tied up with you and the kids and our home."

"So you're saying you want to try again?"

"No, I don't want to try again either. I'm afraid we'll end up making the same old mistakes over and over again."

"So you're saying . . . "

"So I'm saying I don't know what to do." Scott paused, and when he spoke again there was a quiver in his voice, "But I sure could use a friend right now."

The line grew quiet. So much silence after such violent storms. I felt the hotness of familiar tears welling up in my eyes. There he was again. My sixteen-year-old best friend inside my thirty-three-year-old ornery husband. How could I bear to lose this?

When I found my voice, I answered. "Me too. I miss you. Come on home."

"I'll be there in about twenty minutes."

I hung up the phone and ran to the bathroom. I had less than half an hour to get casually knock-'em-dead gorgeous. My husband was coming in for a landing at the family nest. At least, it was a start.

"For I will set My eyes on them for good, and I will bring them again to this land; and I will build them up and not overthrow them, and I will plant them and not pluck them up. And I will give them a heart to know Me, for I am the Lord*; and they will be My people, and I will be their God, for they will return to Me with their whole heart."*

Jeremiah 24:6–7, nasb

EIGHT

The ruckus ain't worth the reward anymore

I have to admit it. Six feet of boots, blue jeans, and denim shirt looked pretty good to me as Scott slowly walked into the house, gently closing the front door behind him. I suppose, after a couple of lonely days and nights, I didn't look too shabby to him either.

Wordless, he took my hand, led me to the bedroom, sat down in the old green rocker, and pulled me to his lap. I nestled my face next to his in that warm spot just under his ear and wrapped my arms around his neck. For a long time we held each other in that position and just rocked and wept. How could we love each other this much and be so miserable at the same time?

I finally let out one of those Grand Finale shuddering sniffs that always follow momentous crying spells, and then I found my voice.

"Scott, I heard something on the radio today that nearly broke me up. Have you ever heard the song, 'What's Forever For?'"

Scott wrinkled his forehead.

"What station did you hear it on?" he asked.

I gave him the call letters then added, "I think it's a brand new station."

Scott shook his head. "What time did you hear it?"

"It was on the way home from school. I guess about 4:45. A few hours before you called tonight. Why?"

"Because I heard the same song at the same time on the same radio station and it had the same effect on me."

"*Somebody* must be trying to tell us something," I whispered.

"Yeah, but what is it?"

"He is saying you're going to have to rock with me a loooooong time, Baby."

"All right," he agreed, "but under one condition."

"What's that?"

"You've gotta switch sides. My right leg's gone numb."

With that touch of humor and the meeting of smiles, we began making up the way we always make up after a big fight. Since this conflict had been what they call a real "humdinger" here in Texas—and such a traumatic thing as "divorce" had been seriously taken into consideration—the making up period was extended accordingly. We both called in sick and spent the entire next day at home.

Well, we *were* sick! Before we took the day off our heads had hurt, our eyes had been swollen and red, and our stomachs had been twisted into painful knots. But it is amazing what staying home and resting will do for a body.

As an aside, when the kids are home we've worked out a secret code for letting them know Mom and Dad would like to be left undisturbed for awhile. Scott tells them, "Your momma and I are worn out. We need to take a little nap. Don't even think about knockin' on our bedroom door unless there's a fire. Even then, make sure the fire is bigger than a breadbox."

The little ones are gullible enough, but the teenage boys have been known to give their father an exaggerated wink and say,

"Suuuure, Dad." I think we need to come up with something a bit more creative than taking a *nap*. But what? Conducting a secret investigation? Developing photographs?

During Open House at Gabe's school last fall, the children had been asked to draw pictures of their daddies. The fathers were to guess which picture was drawn by their own child. It took Scott all of two seconds to find his. Gabe had drawn a man lying on a bed, snoring. The caption read, "My Daddy likes to take LOTS of naps."

As much as physical affection helps, rebounding from a big blowup is a lot like getting over a stomach virus. The patient is tender for awhile, even after the retching is over and the healing has begun. As we began the process of talking about what to do about our volatile relationship, we both agreed on one point: We were getting too old for this. Sure, the passion was always great after a good knock-down-drag-out, but the rewards just weren't worth the agony to either of us anymore.

One evening, not long after the fight, I settled down in my personal library—a hot bathtub full of bubbles—to read my Bible. Once again my eyes settled on a verse that seemed made-to-order for us: "If you keep on biting and devouring each other, watch out or you will be destroyed by each other" (Gal. 5:15).

The words carried the weight of a plea from that Someone who cared deeply about the two of us—the same Someone who had fixed it so that we both heard that "Forever" song at the same time on the same day. The warning was simple: If we continued this pattern, we would eventually eat each other alive. I had a sudden macabre vision of Scott and me taking angry bites out of the other until nothing was left but a pitiful pile of bones.

Something happened in that bathtub full of bubbles that marked the end of an era for me. I realized we were going to have to make some significant changes if we were to survive intact as a couple. And if we were not going to sink or jump ship, we needed to find a way to get the boat turned around.

Look also at ships: although they are so large and are driven by fierce winds, they are turned by a very small rudder wherever the pilot desires.

James 3:4, NKJV

NINE

Is there stop 'n' go counseling for couples on the run?

As Scott and I walked down the thick, carpeted hallway toward the mahogany door marked "Licensed Family Therapists," I fought the urge to run. As people strolled by, I wanted to stop and offer them a word of explanation.

My feelings reminded me of the time I was about seven years old and I could not yet ride my bicycle without training wheels. Desperate to cover my handicap to any window-peeking neighbors, I rode up and down the sidewalk loudly declaring, "I know how to ride this bicycle *without* these training wheels! It's just that my Daddy doesn't know how to take them *off!*"

In much the same way I wanted to shout, "Look, we really don't belong in this psychiatric building! My Sweetie and I are just dropping by for a 1:00 appointment—more like a *visit* really—to tie up a few loose ends. Everything is completely under control. No need to call any white-coated men with straitjackets. It is true that some people do refer to me as a 'fruit cake,' but it is just a little joke."

Instead, I managed a weak smile and put my hand in Scott's for reassurance.

After having talked it over, Scott and I had decided to take Laticia's advice and seek outside assistance. After numerous phone calls to a variety of counselors, one significant psychological truth was already beginning to emerge. This business of getting marriage counseling was going to cost us big bucks. A one-hour session would cost about eighty dollars. And this was supposed to be *good* compared to the prices for mental health in the big city.

I was confident of one thing: Scott and I would have to be fast learners and the therapist a speed talker if we were going to fix our marital problems before we went broke. There could be no whiling away of precious seconds in the therapist's office with idle chitchat. As a matter of fact, I would have preferred the doctors simply tell us what we needed to do to live "happily ever after" in one easy session—and stick any follow-up instructions in a pizza box "to go." Unfortunately, there was no listing under Drive-Through Counseling Services; no Therapy to Go; and most of all, no One-Hour Cure or It's Free.

As Scott leaned against the heavy door to the waiting room, we could hear the strains of savage-beast-calming music pouring from the soothing, omnipresent stereo. I walked in with my head held high, giving the other patients in the waiting room my most impressively sane smile. Then I sank into the pale blue velvet chair beside my husband, took out my notes, and mentally rehearsed what I would tell the therapist.

My imaginary conversation was interrupted by the heart-stopping announcement, "Mr. and Mrs. Freeman, the doctor is ready to see you."

I noted with relief that our therapist was dressed casually—dress slacks, plaid shirt, no tie. He had a kind smile and relaxed demeanor, putting us quickly at ease. As he shook our hands and greeted us pleasantly, most of my apprehension dissipated. However, I did have to keep myself in check as we followed the doctor toward his office. I wanted to blurt out, "Move it, Doc. The clock's a-ticking and, at least in this case, talk ain't cheap!"

As soon as the door to the private office closed behind us, I took charge, planning to move things right along. Talking like an auctioneer, I quickly gave the counselor a verbal synopsis of our problems. Then I let him know I'd be happy to give him summarized notes on any other information he might need in the future.

There was a two-second pause before the counselor answered back. That pause, as you know, represented another nickel—down the drain. I wondered if we could all simply agree to dismiss repetitive phrases, nervous ticks, and prolonged periods of breathing for this one pricey hour. We had a lot of information to exchange if all our problems were to be solved by two o'clock.

Scott and I began our tales of woe, and the counselor eventually shook his head in wonder and probably broke the cardinal rule of marriage counseling by looking shocked.

"You two really don't know how to communicate very well, do you?" he observed.

I was insulted. I knew I could talk a blue streak and Scott had a college degree in communications.

Next, the counselor walked over to a chalkboard on the wall. In the first $20.53 of this session, he gave us a great piece of generic advice. He drew a line down the middle of the board. On one side he wrote the word, *Reacting*. On the other side of the line he wrote the word, *Responding*.

"Scott and Becky, " he coached, "one of your goals here will be to move from the reacting to the responding side of the board." That sounded easy enough. Like a game, perhaps. In the next $15.86 of our time together, it became apparent that we were dealing with issues slightly more complicated than Tiddly-Winks. At this point Scott leaned over and coarsely whispered in my ear.

"Becky, you're embarrassing me. Stop snapping your fingers and saying 'Cut to the chase.'"

I tried to relax, but it was hard not to think of the amount of milk and cereal and ground beef I could buy for *eighty bucks!* I had to remind myself of the fact that we were here to learn. Soon, however, I did begin to wonder when we'd get to the part where the counselor would put Scott in his place and tell him he'd better shape up if he was going to keep the love of a charming, fast-thinking woman like myself.

Instead the therapist turned to my husband and began asking him several questions—how was he feeling, what changes had taken place in his life, what were his expectations of marriage. After $18.46 more of this sort of dialogue I thought, *Well, what am I? Chopped liver?*

But as Scott continued to share, I gradually began to *hear.* I even began to *understand*—how I had knowingly at times, but mostly unknowingly, hurt him. When my turn came to express some of the pain I had also experienced, it was with an immediate sense of relief. Why? Because I could also see that Scott was listening—*really listening*—to my concerns.

Considering the shape we were in, I honestly doubt we would ever have been able to see each other's side of our problems without the help of an official go-between. Incredible perspective can be gained from having a wise, neutral third party involved when the web gets too tangled for two.

In the counseling process, we would eventually learn a variety of techniques for improving communication—some helpful, some hilarious, and some downright humiliating. My absolute favorite is a technique I actually invented myself. I'm pleased to announce that I'm still using it with excellent results. As a matter of fact, this very afternoon I received a letter from a young mother of three whose husband is in the Air Force, serving in Saudi Arabia. She asked permission to borrow this technique to try on her husband when he hits American soil. I thought the device might bear repeating here since it seems to be on the cutting edge of therapeutic advancement. I call it the "Help Your Man Meet Your Needs Technique," and this is how it works:

Whenever I find myself in need of a hug or words of affection, I locate Scott and put my arms around his neck.

Then I say, "You think I'm so sweet and pretty you can hardly keep your eyes off me, don't you?" He can't resist a smile and obediently nods. I am fulfilled and happy. Actually, he reports that my putting words in his mouth causes him to realize he really does feel the words. So I am working on this line next: "Scott, you just love cute, nicely-rounded women. You'd hate to see me lose an ounce, wouldn't you, Sweetheart?"

Even with the good advice we'd received on our first day, I am sorry to report that we were unable to tie up all the "loose ends" of our marriage in one easy lesson. Scott and I would be back at the counselor's office several more times that spring. And I must also admit that all the sessions did not end as warmly as the first. Once we both walked out of the building and raced toward our separate cars. Then, with tires squealing and rubber burning, we each pulled out of the parking lot as fast as we could drive—in opposite directions. Maturity under pressure has never been one of our strong points.

Another time, Scott went to a session without me. Once, I also went alone. On yet another occasion, we both left the counselor's office hurting so badly that he insisted on a morning-after follow-up session just to make sure we each made it through the night. There was no way to avoid some pain. As I've said, it hurts to get our boxes tipped over—to clean out all the junk inside a relationship. It hurts to get the needle on our records bumped out of familiar grooves. And the intermediate sounds aren't always pleasant either. At least not until the needle finally settles onto some new bands of beautiful music. Because of this experience, I've come to a new understanding of a passage from Hosea that has always bothered me: "Come, let us return to the Lord. He has torn us to pieces but he will heal us; he has injured us but he will bind up our wounds" (Hosea 6:1).

Why would God intentionally wound those He loved? Was it some kind of cruel game? The more I come to know the Wonderful Counselor, the more I realize that there are times when He has to break us down in order to heal us. And as I read the entire story of Hosea, it is obvious that God takes no joy in the tearing-down process. Like a surgeon who must cut in order to heal, God occasionally has to make painful incisions in our hearts that will eventually allow us to live life more fully and with greater joy and freedom than we ever imagined.

As I finish this chapter, it is dark and quiet. The only light in the house comes from my computer screen. Kids are tucked in bed. Scott's on his way home from a visit with his folks. All is well. So well, in fact, that my cup—and my eyes—runneth over with gratitude.

If by chance there is a man or a woman reading these pages whose marriage is out of control, may I stop here for a moment—right here in the middle of this page—and encourage you as Laticia and her husband encouraged us? Perhaps you may be led to a counselor, a pastor, a book or a tape, or a wise and trusted friend. But begin to look, as you pray—there *are* great sources available for aching relationships.

It is ironic that we human beings are trained for almost every conceivable skill in life, but most of us are never really taught the dynamics of human interaction. And there's a lot to learn. If two people have the desire to make a marriage work and are willing to combine action with that desire, a good relationship is possible. Not perfect—but good. If Scott and I hadn't made the long walk down that hall, pushed open the mahogany door labeled "Licensed Family Therapists," and sacrificed some hefty grocery money, we might not be happily crunching our cornflakes in unison today.

One of the most poignant quotes I've ever read about the process of giving and receiving help comes from the book *When a Leader Falls.* The book is thoughtfully written by two friends of mine, Deb Frazier and Jan Winebrenner, and is published by Bethany House. They wrote:

> We all like being the one who is able to give, who has all the answers and has everything under control . . . . But God doesn't allow any of us the comfort of such a role indefinitely. We need Him, and we need one another. We all are destined to do time on the bottom of some heap. At any given moment there exists within the body those who need assistance and those who can provide it and the players are constantly changing.[1]

Scott and I have been on the bottom of a few heaps. And hopefully, we'll help pull a couple of fellow travelers up off the bottom of theirs along the way. No one has it all together, but I'm convinced that is exactly why we need each other. Life has its way of forcing us to take turns. No one is immune to struggles and trials. But when the Lord has granted us hope and healing, it's a joy and privilege to comfort others in their time of need.

If only you could be here tonight when my husband comes in the door—if you could see the friendship, the love, the spark between us now. How we'll hold each other close and talk into the night even though we know we need to get to sleep. And if you could have seen the mess we had made of our marriage only a few short years ago, you would appreciate what God, our Good Shepherd, has done.

Perhaps I love picturing Christ as my personal Shepherd because I have always found my greatest comfort in the Twenty-third Psalm: It seems to have a universal application to every conceivable human ache. I wonder how many millions of frightened men, women, and children have been wrapped, like a cozy warm quilt, in David's comforting words?

Often the Shepherd led me through the dark valley with the light of His Word. Other times it was through the spoken and written counsel of wise men and women who'd already trudged through this sort of darkness and could now help others navigate rocky terrain. Because of where Scott and I have been, the green pastures we are enjoying tonight are incredibly precious to me. Not that we've completely "arrived," by any means. The chapters to come will make that more than clear. And there will probably be some more dark valleys to cross when we will feel hurt, lost, and confused again. But as we cry for help, I now know—deep in my soul—He will *always* find us and He will *always* lead us home. That's what our Shepherd is for.

Because the Lord is my Shepherd, I have everything I need! He lets me rest in the meadow grass and leads me beside the quiet streams . . . . Even when walking through the dark valley of death I will not be afraid, for you are close beside me, guarding, guiding all the way.

PSALM 23:1–2, 4, TLB

TEN

After I walked a mile in his shoes, his feet didn't smell so bad

Shortly after we had called 911 to rescue our marriage, we went to Florida for vacation. We had five days with nothing to do but lie on the white, sandy beaches by the majestic ocean, bask in the sun, swim, and eat. Scott, especially, needed it.

He had taken an extra job remodeling a house so our family could enjoy this quality time together. We'd even graduated from marriage counseling. Then "why come" (as my kids used to say) were my husband and I not speaking to each other—again?

Scott had been gone so much before we left for this trip that by the time we had crammed the last beach umbrella and floatie into the van and settled into the front seats for the trip, I was looking over at a man who seemed more like a stranger. Was any vacation worth the amount of time we had spent apart these weeks? Could any trip, no matter how exciting, be worth watching my poor husband drag his aching, exhausted body home night after night while the kids asked me, "Do you think we'll ever get to see Daddy standing up with his eyes open again?"

I begged Scott to give it up—we'd stay home, go to Six Flags over Texas and stay in a local hotel this year. But my husband's brown eyes could see nothing but deep blue. Captain Scott *would* take his family to the sea. Come you-know-what or high water. Both possibilities now loomed imminent.

Driving sixteen hours with four kids in a fully packed, loudly reverberating van was not particularly conducive to meaningful dialogue. Scott and I managed to be on our best behavior—at least at the outset of the trip. Our small talk consisted of the usual polite conversation starters.

"How was your day, Honey?"

"Great. And yours? Hey, do you think it might be fun to let the children stop and play at the next rest area? Maybe we could even have a little family picnic?"

So far, so good. But somewhere between Louisiana and Mississippi, our courteous parley began to suffer somewhat.

"What do you mean you're tired of driving, Becky? You haven't even left the off ramp yet!!"

"Would you rather I ruin our whole vacation because I fell asleep at the wheel?!?"

Somewhere between Alabama and Florida we began reserving communication for only the most basic of human needs—and then it was a rather sketchy pantomime affair played out with grunts, scowls, and shrugs. The back end of the van, loaded with four wide-awake and cranky kids, was on the verge of mutiny. Captain Scott's crew was about to sink before we even hit water.

We survived the van voyage only a little worse for wear. And now here I was on the vacation of our dreams. Unfortunately, it had fallen my lot to entertain my own sad and miserable self on this lonely stretch of beach. Scott had long since walked with the kids farther down shore to take them fishing. As a matter of fact, my family was now fishing as *far away* from my resting place as possible while still technically remaining in the same state.

I sighed audibly and pulled out the reading material I had stuffed into my beach bag. Then I stretched out on a towel, preparing to dive into, and hopefully to lose myself in, the paperback I'd retrieved. I looked at the cover and moaned. The letters that stared back at me tauntingly declared: *What Men Really Want* by Herb Goldberg. *Great,* I thought, *just what I'm dying to know.* My initial reaction was, *What am I supposed to get out of this?* But then I remembered the reason the book was in my possession in the first place.

My friend Kathy had given me the book. Her husband, Greg, had given it to her on the occasion of their separation, hoping Kathy might understand that so many of his behaviors were just typical of most men. If she had understood, he thought, maybe she wouldn't have expected so much. Maybe she wouldn't be filing for divorce. Maybe he wouldn't be coming home to an empty, quiet apartment and dying inside with loneliness. Sadly, Kathy was beyond trying—the marriage was over. Still for some reason, she thought *I* might get something out of this book, so she tucked it in my hand before I left.

I sat reading that horrible book in the Florida sun for two days, forcing myself to swallow the bitter pill of learning how a "traditional" man thinks and functions. I often argued out loud with the author.

"Who do you think you are? What's a woman supposed to do? Just suppress all her needs and give 100 percent to the man?!"

However, about halfway through the book, my defenses started to drop and I began to *listen* to what I was reading, praying for an understanding spirit. It was one of those significant turning points, at which I look back and say profoundly, "That was a *Significant* Turning Point."

I realized, and finally came to the point of accepting, the different ways men and women react to each other. I'd probably heard them before at one of those "Ten Ways to Merry Matrimony" seminars, but this time I understood.

First of all, it finally dawned on me that men do not respond to tears and hurt feelings as many women would expect. When most men see a Ball of Female Emotions rolling in their direction they tend to have one of two responses: duck or brace for impact. When their distraught wives come at them, arms flung out for a reassuring embrace, tears flying in all directions like one of those backyard Water Wiggles gone mad, the natural male response is fight or flight. It took seventeen years for me to accept this, and it happened that day on the beach.

In addition, I discovered that men are physically *made* to handle conflict that way. In one study, scientists hooked men and women up to some wires that would test their responses during a confrontation. Now, I suspect men and women the world over have fantasized about hooking each other up to electrical wires during fights, but under scientific control, the results were amazing.

The study showed that a man's emotions were much more intense during a conflict than those of a woman. In other words, a man's boiling point came when the woman was still on a slow simmer. To avoid lashing out and boiling over, the man shuts down. Meanwhile, the woman is still wanting to duke this thing out and has the intense desire to continue fighting until a resolution can be found or until she at least gets a reassuring hug. (Which, if the truth were told, is usually the resolution she is seeking in the first place.)

"So *that's* it!" I said aloud there on the beach, feeling a strange sense of relief.

As a member of the gentler sex, all I knew was that the best way for a person to gain *my* sympathy was to cry. I also knew instinctively what to do to help a friend in pain. I'd put my arms around the poor girl and let her cry it out. Then I'd sympathize with the victim's pitiful plight and let her talk until she felt better or until we finished the cheesecake.

When Scott and I were newly married, the day came when he inevitably hurt my feelings. I, a product of centuries of genteel Southern breeding, grabbed my hanky and turned on my body's automatic estrogen-propelled sprinkler system. I do declare, my gentleman husband's response just nearly gave me the vapors. I was *completely* dumbfounded that my hero didn't respond with pats and hugs and "I'm sorrys." I couldn't believe he could be so callous and cold. Not a *sliver* of cheesecake did he offer to console my aching heart.

Using female logic, I came to one conclusion: I must not be communicating with enough *intensity.* So I cranked up the volume and increased the melodrama. Same response. Scott would take a hike or brace for a fight. Each year I added a more spectacular technique to try to gain Scott's affection. I'm too proud to admit some of them, but let me just say we've replaced a few dishes and patched a few nicks in the walls as a result of those failed experiments.

Again, it was the same song, zillionth verse: Fight or Flight. Finally, I hit on an astounding gem of truth. "More of the same is not going to do the trick," I told myself. "You can cry for sympathy for the next forty years, Becky, and you can bet your darlin' dentures that your old wrinkled-up husband will be leaving just as fast as he can get his wheelchair out the door."

That's when I discovered the second Amazing Secret: The best thing I can do to break up a stalemate in an argument is usually the *exact opposite* of what I naturally feel like doing. When I feel like launching into a screaming rage, that's my clue to stay especially calm and collected. At this point I need to use all the powers of the Holy Spirit available to me to respond with dignity and decorum. Of course, when this happens, it's truly miraculous. (It's not in my makeup to be naturally dignified or decorumed.) If I have an overpowering urge to fight it out "right here, right now, to the finish," that's my signal to take a walk and cool off instead.

"Isn't that denial?" you may ask. "Stuffing your feelings that need to be released?" Glad you asked.

I don't think so. It's less about pretending natural emotions don't exist and more about self-control and redirecting. Proverbs 29:11 kept coming back to my mind in those days: "A fool gives full vent to his anger." Even psychologists are beginning to question the wisdom of "letting all your inward anger out." If this practice is carried on for too long, they are finding it actually increases rather than decreases violent feelings. I'm no psychologist; I just want results, and this approach seems to work much better for me.

Still, there's the problem of what to do with my jumbled emotions and pain when Scott has managed, either intentionally or unintentionally, to temporarily break my heart. Mind you, I still have my crying spell if I'm up to it. After all, it's my pity party. But I usually host it alone now and ask the Lord to be my Comforter. I may get together with a trusted friend who lets me cry on her shoulder and is known to keep rich dessert in her kitchen. When I'm quite finished, I dry my tears and get on with doing something I love doing until the timing is right, both of our tempers have cooled, and we're ready to take a first stab at reconciling.

Notice I say "first" stab. Usually it takes more than one attempt, but I know now to just keep waiting and gingerly testing the waters before one of us attempts the final, once-and-for-all "making-up talk." If Scott's still angry, I'm learning to just leave it alone and get busy doing something else I enjoy instead. Maybe I'll go for a cup of coffee and browse at a bookstore, have lunch with the girls, take a walk in the woods, or go to the mall for some intensive shopping therapy. Anything but mull and stew!

On one occasion I took the kids and checked into a motel for the day. Had a ball. It got me away from the scene of the crime so that I wouldn't lose my dignity or say things I regretted. Now at those times of conflict, I still have a little ache in my stomach. It reminds me that all is not well between me and the man I love. I miss the sauce—the "gravy," if you will—of romantic feelings. But better to deal with the pain constructively and wait patiently for the right timing than to blow pieces of each other's emotions all over the place. That way there's less mess to forgive when all is calm on the homefront again.

I can't tell you what a difference this change in attitude made almost immediately. That day in Florida I put the book down, and since I'd already used up the first forty-eight hours of my vacation going about in sackcloth and ashes, I decided I might as well enjoy all that I could salvage of the rest of it. A full day had not passed before Scott noticed I was actually having a good time without him. Since it was totally out of character for me to act "normal" when I've been upset, it got his attention—and attracted him like a bee to honey.

One night toward the end of the week, Scott and I walked hand in hand on the beach and had a long talk. He asked about my sudden change of heart, and I told him I was finished with falling to pieces trying to gain his attention. I could see the visible relief on his face as he heaved a sigh. Then I told him I forgave him for being a man. I could see visible signs of confusion on his face.

"Huh?" he began.

But before he could say anything, I added a P. S. "Scott, I just want you to know that when I'm having an emotional day or you've hurt my feelings and you don't want to deal with it, I have to have some way to cope. I'm trying to look to God to supply the love I need, but I may need to talk with a friend. I may need to get away from the house. I may need a Gold Card."

He started to protest, but then, from a sidewalk cafe in the distance, we heard the strains of the classic beach song "Boardwalk." I smiled up into my husband's handsome face, and even in the moonlight I could see his eyes sparkle mischievously. Without a word, he grabbed me by the waist and twirled me around with expert ease before landing me back in a romantic dip and planting one of those *Gone with the Wind* kisses on my lips. As you can see, making up is one of our fortes. We've had a lot of practice. Of course, music and stars and waves didn't hurt the mood either.

All the work and late hours Scott had put in to get us to this moment by the sea with these brilliant stars overhead seemed suddenly worthwhile. I melted deeper into my sea-lovin' husband's arms, savoring the night wind, moonlight, and seagulls' call. Closing my eyes, I pondered our rocky, weird relationship.

Scott and I may never understand fully how the opposite sex really thinks, I decided. *But right now*—as I rested my head on my Captain's chest and squeezed him close—*I couldn't care less. Right here, for at least tonight, I'm gonna get smothered in gravy.*

In quietness and in confidence shall be your strength.

Isaiah 30:15, KJV

ELEVEN

Send an sos for pms—asap!

When Gabriel was in first grade, he came home from school complaining about the behavior of a certain little boy who sat in the desk next to him.

"Mom," he moaned, "this is the whiniest kid I ever saw. I mean, *nobody* can do anything to make him happy! All he does is gripe, gripe, gripe—*all day long!* Really, he's got the worst case of PMS I've ever *seen* in a kid."

Obviously, Gabriel had learned that whatever PMS meant, it was bad news, but he didn't quite have all the details worked out. I struggled to keep a straight face and informed Gabriel that boys do not get PMS. Later I happened upon an entry in Gabe's journal, apparently written after he had had a battle with his big brother, Zachary. It read: "I jest had sum thing ownlee girls have. PMS WITH ZACHARY FREEMAN!"

Poor kid, now I had him worried about his sexual identity, so his father decided it was time for a man-to-man talk.

"Son," he told him, "don't worry about trying to understand women or PMS. I'm thirty-six years old and I'm more confused than ever. I've learned one thing after living with your mother and working in an office with fifty-two women. When you see a woman coming toward you who says she's having 'one of those days,' get ready to duck, run, or hand her a fistful of Kleenex."

Even the teenagers in our house are skittish at certain times of the month. During one particularly stress-filled, premenstrual week, I did not get the help I felt I needed to bring the groceries in from the car, so of course, as I hauled a gallon jug of milk from the car, I threw it against the wall of the entry hall like most mothers do. Boy, did I regret *that* little burst of temper. A few weeks later, I was again bringing in the groceries and I asked the boys to get up and help me unload the car. Zeke started to complain, but just in time, Zach—older and wiser—intervened.

"Hey, Zeke, better jump up and salute. Mom's standing near dairy products."

We laugh about PMS because laughing is at least one way to cope with it.

I had finally recognized a pattern in my life that *had* to be related to PMS. For two or three days of each month, my whole world seemed to turn black. I could think of no reason during those days to put one foot in front of the other. All of life seemed bleak. Only a few days before, my family seemed charming and lovable. Suddenly they turned into hideous imbeciles. I found myself fighting the urge to growl and bite! And what mental image did I conjure up of myself during this week? A fat, ugly one.

When Scott and I really thought about our up-and-down relationship over the years, we finally began to realize that we usually had a fairly big blowup about once a month. I don't know—call it genius—but after seventeen years we began to wonder if there might be a correlation between the angry fights and the flux of my hormones. Well, what do you know? There was. As a matter of fact, we could set our watches to the times when it would be best to run, duck, or hide the dairy products.

I now wonder how many of our revolving conflicts were due to a drop in estrogen rather than a drop in communication? It was so hard for me to believe that part of our problems might be related to premenstrual syndrome that I strongly denied it for years. How I hated the thought of being patronized simply for being a woman with a hormonal cycle!

Our conversations often reminded me of a scene from the sitcom *Cheers*, when the articulate and emotional Diane vehemently explodes at Sam.

"I hate you with the white hot heat of a thousand suns!"

Sam calmly responds to her furious statement with a singsong version of "Somebody's crank-y."

That sort of response from Scott was about as effective as throwing Texas chili on a fire to try to extinguish the flames. But to his everlasting credit, he was the first to entertain the thought that hormones might be affecting my attitude. It had first dawned on Scott the night of our birthday shoot-out at the Trail Dust. At that point he learned to do what all successful husbands eventually learn to do. He consciously chose to not take my moods so personally, at least not before checking the calendar. In the bouts that followed before I got around to seeing a gynecologist, I insisted there were substantial reasons for my anger, but he kept his resolve. After a few more months of denial, I began to think about the possibility that PMS was a real problem and it had greatly affected our relationship.

Two days later I was sitting alone in my doctor's examining room, tissue in hand, crying over a picture in a magazine. It was a fuzzy portrait of a mother nursing her newborn infant. *Oh, that's so sweet. I remember how precious my babies were. Now I'm all out of babies. I'll never hold a newborn of my own again.* I flipped the page and saw a recipe for a chocolate Easter bunny cake. Fresh sobs began to flow as I remembered the bunny cake my mother had baked for my fifth birthday. *I loved that cake!* On the opposite side of the page was an ad for Charmin toilet paper. *Oh, how Nonnie used to love Charmin toilet paper. And*

Dove soap too. I miss her so much! It was all too much. And just then, my gynecologist rounded the corner and glanced at my tears and tissue.

"Let me guess," she said, stroking her chin. "Hormones acting up a bit these days?" Over the top of my tissue my red eyes blinked affirmatively. Once inside her office, we discussed all the options available for coping with PMS.

"Becky," she gently informed me, "after about age thirty—and especially after having had multiple children—premenstrual syndrome often becomes more pronounced. "

"Well," I deadpanned, "in my situation PMS is pronounced like a four-letter word."

She smiled. "There are some things you can do. A change in diet may help. You probably ought to cut out caffeine and chocolate."

"Life without *coffee* and *chocolate?*" I asked. I had not realized how serious my condition was!

I noticed the doctor ease away from me ever so slightly. She also moved a large hypodermic needle out of my reach before she continued. "Another medical alternative is to take a non-addictive mild antidepressant—only on the days when PMS is acting up. Also, a good multivitamin with lots of B6 and calcium would be advisable."

"I can go for that," I sighed.

Today my entire family would like to line up and applaud this doctor. Even though I only take the prescription about three days a month, it has made a tremendous difference. I don't really know how to describe the change, except to say that instead of screaming and throwing jugs of milk, I might only raise my voice slightly and twist the lid on the jug more tightly than usual. I now deal with a controllable irritation instead of a tidal wave.

I found another huge help in a book by Jean Lush called *Emotional Phases of a Woman's Life.* I especially appreciated her candor when she talked about her own experience with PMS. "I was horrified to think that someone would uncover my terrible dark secret. How could I ever manage to live a life of service to God when, for three or four days out of the month, I turned into a monster? Eventually I learned that I was not a freak of nature, as I had suspected. For years I thought I was somehow different, perhaps even crazy. I'd look around at other women, and they would seem to have themselves all together."[1]

What a relief to know someone else had battled the same feelings! Though Scott is not a great reader of self-help books—especially about women—he did read the first few chapters in *Emotional Phases of a Woman's Life*. It was enormously helpful for him—especially the part where Mrs. Lush describes a typical woman in a typical monthly cycle. He thought he was reading my autobiography.

Two other approaches have been especially helpful to us. Women who suffer from PMS should prepare for the Big Event by keeping the calendar as free from stress as possible. I call it cocooning. For those dreadful one or two days out of the month, I allow myself to lie back, wrap up in a blanket, and take long naps if I feel like it. My hot baths are longer, my walks more leisurely. Rather than tackle the deep books I usually enjoy, I may read mindless magazine fluff and watch a lighthearted comedy. I simply don't expect much out of myself, and my family has been kind enough to do the same.

In addition, Scott has taken a slightly more "parental approach," and at times it works fairly well. When I am displaying some "missed-nap" grumpiness, Scott has learned to simply take me gently in his arms. Sometimes he will even lead me by the hand to the bedroom and, even while I'm protesting, stretch me out on the bed, cover me with a comforter, kiss my furrowed brow, and walk calmly away, shutting the door firmly behind him.

Then he barricades it for three days.

A couple of months ago, my sister Rachel called from Virginia Beach. I could immediately tell she was fighting back tears.

"Becky," she began, "this is a hard phone call for me to make, but Mom said you'd understand. I think I'm losing it! In the parking lot today at the mall, a van was waiting for my parking place. I was trying to get Trevor buckled in his car seat and they started *honking* at me. Suddenly, I was absolutely *livid!* About five mafia-type guys unloaded from the van, but at that point, I didn't care if they *were* the mafia. I wagged my finger at them and roared, 'You boys need to learn some manners!'

"When I finally got home and calmed down, I realized that I could have put Trevor and myself in a dangerous situation just because of my temper. It scared me to death."

I had to laugh at the picture of my "very together" sister shaking her finger at some rough, gang member-types and telling them to mind their manners. "So what time of the month is it?" I inquired. Care to guess what her answer was?

I overnighted her a copy of Jean Lush's book and the phone number of a couple of information lines and warned her to avoid carrying any dairy products for the time being. (By the way, if you're having a real emergency, and that cup of yogurt is about to be airborne, PMS Access is 1-800-222-4PMS and PMS Relief is 916-888-7677.)

Last night we talked again. She'd been to the doctor and was also finding many of her worst symptoms alleviated. She had found a natural herbal remedy, along with high potency vitamin and mineral tablets of calcium, magnesium, and a multiple B. They seem to work well for her. It made me feel wonderful to know that I might have been able to pass on some help and encouragement to my sister. She's so often done the same for me in other areas. We talked about how many of our women friends also struggle with serious bouts of monthly tension.

So I'd like to dedicate this chapter to my sister and all you fellow sisters out there who are searching for and trying new ways to cope with PMS in your lives and in your marriages. My prayers are with you. (Scott says *his* prayers are with your *husbands*.)

As a matter of fact, why don't we all go to the fridge right now, grab a large jug of milk, take off the lid, and raise it in a toast. Here's to us, the Survivors of the Hormone Onslaught! Now take a swig right out of the jug (go ahead, the kids aren't looking). Let's all say "Ahhhh . . . " while we wipe the mustache from our upper lips with the back of our hands in triumph. Finally, I think we should pat ourselves on the back for having the amazing self-control not to throw the container against the wall. We women need to take small victories whenever we can find them.

"I have told you these things, so that in me you may have peace. In this world you will have trouble. But take heart! I have overcome the world."

JOHN 16:33

TWELVE

It's a guy thing

In addition to responding to conflict differently, I've noticed one or two other basic differences between the male and the female of our species. For the better part of seven years, I carried at least one child in my womb. The experience gifted me with stretch marks down to my ankles. I clean up after their stomach viruses, await their beck and call for chauffeur services, listen sympathetically to their stories, and soothe their hurt feelings. You can often find me, bleary-eyed and martyr-like, typing their book reports after 11:00 P.M. Even so, they rarely seem to notice my sacrifices. I've been taking an informal inventory this week, and here is a sampling of the comments I've received from my children concerning my few *flaws*—flaws which they seem intent upon magnifying.

1. "MOM! This is a ditch, not a driveway! You are *nuts!*"

2. "You mean even after I left a note scotch-taped to your nightgown last night you *still* forgot to put those jeans in the dryer?! Now I have to wear the ones with a *hole* in the leg?!???"

3. "The battery's dead in the smoke alarm again, Mom. I guess after you burn *three* cobblers in a row, it takes its toll on the ol' Energizers."

(Yeah, but one of those cobblers bubbled up and burned into the shape of Jimmy Durante's nose, and we even saved it to show the neighbors. Not just every old mom burns food with flair.)

To be fair, I also received a few hugs and dutiful pecks on the cheek at bedtime, even a couple of "thank-yous" thrown in for good measure. But I'd truly love for someone to explain why the *father* of my children can simply walk into the house, put down his briefcase, grunt "Hi kids—howyadoing," and all four offspring nearly hyperventilate trying to be the first to get close to him. They are crazy about this man, and all he has to do is stroll into a room and breathe. It's been a phenomenon I've enjoyed observing as I mull over the things that keep me loving this man to whom I am married.

To my way of thinking, this whole masculine phenomenon is sort of a throwback from old Clint Eastwood movies. I'm sure we all remember how much effort Eastwood put into his intimate relationships (at least his pre-*Bridges of Madison County* days. As I recall, Clint spent—on average—one hundred and ten minutes of a two-hour movie chasing bad guys, stopping only briefly to sneer into the camera. He didn't give a thought to his girlfriend all day long, much less contemplate giving her a call to let her know he might be running a little late. Yet when he finished allowing his quota of criminals to "make his day," he simply sauntered into a scene, gave a pitiful excuse for a wink—which was more like a wince, really—and waited for his leggy Insignificant Other to fall helplessly into his arms. And amazingly, she did it! What's the deal?!?

Scott tells me it's "A Guy Thing"—the masculine *mystique* that attracts women and children to a man with magnetic, invisible charm. Although I admit there must be something to that theory, there are a few other "Guy Things" that don't exactly ooze with "mystiquey," magnetic charm.

Just out of curiosity, have you ever noticed how a man orders food at a fast-food drive-through window? First of all, I've come to believe that the mere sound of a masculine voice causes the ordering equipment to suffer a nervous breakdown, thereafter eliminating all possibilities for meaningful communication. Add to that the fact that men have an innate desire to be *cute* while placing their order through the drive-through microphone. It's as if they believe the invisible mike on the plastic menu screen is actually connected to a standup comedy stage somewhere in the recesses of the restaurant. But when their cute antics backfire, men are surprisingly offended. Here's an example of a conversation between my man and a typical fast-food machine.

"Hello, welcome to Royal Burger. Can I help you please?"

"I don't know. Can you?"

"May I take your order now, sir?"

"Well, of course you *may*. But should you do it today or tomorrow? That is the question."

(Long period of silence. Scott winks at me as if to say, "Watch me have a little fun with this character.")

"Did you say 'cut the mayo and hold the tomato,' sir?" the voice continues, and by the sound of it, I get the feeling he's handled wanna-be comedians before.

This is where the waiter turns to a fellow employee and winks as if to say, "Watch me have some fun with this jerk."

And Scott, still thinking he is in control, persists. "Cut the mayo on what? I haven't ordered yet!"

"Do you want fries with that?"

"Wait a minute! With that *what?*"

"Will that be a small, medium, large, or jumbo super saver, sir?"

"WAIT, WAIT, WAIT!" Scott now is babbling. "I'm not talking to a stupid machine anymore. Hey, look—I can see the *real you* from here if you'll take a peek out of your little window! Well, you can just read my lips: Hasta la vista, baby! I'm outta of here!" As we peel away with tires screeching, we can hear the invisible waiter droning patiently through the speaker.

"Yes, sir. Do you want some fries with that, sir?"

I've got to hand it to them. They don't call them fast-food employees for nothing. Those kids are pretty quick on the draw.

There's yet another "Guy Thing" that puzzles me. Why is it that grown men, who would shudder at the thought of going off to war, will risk their lives to avoid admitting they need help on a home improvement project? Currently, my husband is building a huge, two-story shell over our small cabin—by himself. It is turning out to be very much like a Hollywood stage front, actually. To people driving by, it looks as though we live in a large home like the one owned by June and Ward Cleaver. Inside, however, the original small cabin still stands, with our family running about like six hamsters in a five-gallon aquarium.

A couple of weeks ago, Scott decided to caulk the upper corner of the gable end on our new roof. Now, I might mention that the peak on this outer roof is twenty-eight feet above ground. Unfortunately, Scott's scaffolding was just shy of allowing him to reach the peak, so he decided to take his caulk gun in hand and jump for it. Obviously, this was a *Man-Made Decision.*

The Man managed to leap high enough to grasp the top corner of the roof with his left hand, the caulk gun ready to fire in his right. Glancing down, he quickly discovered he was no longer hanging *above* the scaffolding, but had swung out away from the house and several feet away from the scaffold. In other words, Scott was dangling twenty-eight feet above the ground, holding on for dear life by one hand. Of course, we can all be thankful he had a caulk gun in his other hand for that special, added sense of security.

No one was home that afternoon except Scott and Gabe, our youngest and smallest son, so calling for help was not an option. I later learned that my husband made a flying leap back to safety, achieving a one-point landing on a small two-by-four board which, happily, lay across a section of rickety scaffolding. Thank God for those years Scott had spent in gymnastics in his younger days! It goes without saying that I often pray for angels to watch diligently over my husband—especially when he's doing one of his "Guy Things."

For He will give His angels charge concerning you,
to guard you in all your ways.

PSALM 91:11, NASB

THIRTEEN

Letting the tides of forgiveness wash away old pain

The other day I talked with my editor, and she told me of a frightening new trend in marriage counseling. The new theory is that marriage is so often doomed to failure that it is better to simply look at a first wedding as a stepping-stone, a practice ground for the next marriage. In other words, you make all the mistakes on the first relationship and then walk away—leaving a junk heap of ruined love—and start fresh with someone else. (What if we held this theory with our firstborn children???)

I thought about this new approach and then I answered, "Vicki, you know, the sad part in all of this is that the same starting-over approach can take place within the original marriage instead. At several strategic points, Scott and I basically reintroduced ourselves, shook hands, and began again."

The only hitch in starting over within the original relationship is this: What do we do with this junk heap of mistakes we've made? We have to find a way to deal with all of the grudges that accumulate over the years. How tempting it sounds at times to walk away from it all and fall into the arms of someone new who doesn't know I look like a small underground animal in the mornings. But eventually, I know I'd discover the "new and improved husband" would have a few obnoxious surprises for me too. Maybe he'd pick his toenails and belch while he watched television. I don't know what form it would take, but I know enough about human nature to know it would be *something.*

Unless people plan to spend their lives starting over with new relationships when the old one wears out, the junk will eventually have to be faced and periodically swept out. And actually, that is a great definition of forgiveness—sweeping the old junk off the porch and starting anew.

Easier said than done, I know. There were some things that Scott had done and said that cut so deep, that seemed so unfair and hurtful, that I thought at the time I would never get over them. (And I'm sure the reverse is true for him.) But even if we are wronged unjustly, God asks us to forgive just as He has forgiven us. Ouch. And if God were to weigh the scales with me, I'd come up pitifully short. That's why I need more than everyday grace. I need the *amazing* brand. And it's that same amazing grace and forgiveness our loved ones need from us. I'll be the first to admit we are talking about a supernatural phenomenon here. There's no way we can forgive others without His Spirit working in us.

It also helped me to understand that holding a grudge hurts no one but myself. All the psychology books say that grudges physically inhibit the production of seratonin, a chemical essential for a sense of well-being. Listen, I need all of *that* stuff God designed to come my way. I don't want to stand in the way of a natural, sense-of-well-being chemical invading my body, especially while I'm working on the delicate task of improving relationships.

The process of letting go of anger and applying forgiveness is rarely accomplished overnight, although that does happen on occasion. Forgiveness, for me, was a gradual process. It was much like cleaning away a grimy old film from a pane of glass. As the glass became clear, I could see more and more of the goodness in our relationship. I wrote the following poem in a journal describing some of the feelings I had during the letting-go process.

Oh, now I remember Our Love
Sometimes it comes in gentle waves
Tugging at the lonely beach
Which was
For a time
My heart
Now and again, monumental whitecaps
Spill onto shore
Flowing back to sea
With the debris
Of antique hurt
Yes, I remember Our Love.

BECKY FREEMAN © 1991

I seem to continue dipping back into the sea for metaphors that paint living portraits of love's inner workings. At least I'm in good company. For ages, poets and writers have been drawn to the ocean as they struggle to describe the majestic, strong, unpredictable, cleansing, soothing, healing qualities of love. I especially like this oceanfront view of forgiveness.

I have to admit it was scary to let go of some of my old broken shells of hurt and let them ride out with the waves. They had taken time to collect, to arrange in order from tiny sand-dollar hurts to major conch-shell pains. Perhaps I was struggling to save the old shells in case I needed them for some future "Show and Tell." However, I am reminded of Marlene Dietrich's words: "Once a woman has forgiven her man, she must not reheat his sins for breakfast." Letting go means *letting go.*

And letting go, without grasping for old grievances again, is what we eventually did. As Scott and I rode out with the new tide of love and forgiveness, I must confess that the adventure of sailing in the wide open sea made that isolated beach full of shattered shells seem dull indeed. But I can't say it was easy, especially at first.

As I realized how difficult it was for us to do the necessary "letting go"—the slate-cleaning, broom-sweeping, tide-washing sort of forgiveness it takes to hold a marriage together—I noticed something else taking place on the side. I began to view through more understanding eyes of compassion my close friends whose marriages had floundered.

"For I will forgive . . . and will remember their sins no more." This is what the L*ORD* *says . . . who stirs up the sea so that its waves roar.*

JEREMIAH 31:34–35

F O U R T E E N

Divorce busters anonymous

Some of my best friends are divorced. Actually, all of my best friends are divorced. Well, that's an exaggeration. But I *have* had the painful experience of watching three of my best friends' marriages crumble. I'm talking best, best, best friends—deeply committed Christian friends. I know it's selfish of me to whine when it is my *friends* who have really done the suffering, but whine I must. Friends of the "splitting-up victims" are oft-ignored casualties. At least it's been true with me, because in most cases I felt as if my own heart was pulled in two. And it hurt.

If there had been a recovery group for Friends of Couple Friends Who Suddenly Aren't Couples Anymore, I'd have been first in line on at least three occasions. And now that the specter of divorce had brushed so frighteningly close to us, I thought of our divorced friends more often, and with a lot more empathy.

The other day at lunch I asked a group of married gals, "How did you feel the first time you found out a close friend was getting a divorce?" I expected to hear them say, "Devastated."

Or, "Afraid for them. But afraid for us, too. Because if it could happen to *them,* who's to say it couldn't happen to us?" Or perhaps, "I wanted to console them, but I didn't know which one to comfort without appearing to be taking sides."

The answers I got instead were surprising:

"I never really knew anyone very well who was going through a divorce."

"Oh, I felt bad. But I never thought for a second it could happen to us."

"We grew distant from our divorcing friends. We didn't stay in touch because—you know, they were *single* again. I didn't think they really wanted to hang out with married couples anymore."

I shook my head in disbelief. It was pretty awkward admitting to this group of happily married women that most of my closest friends eventually ended up in a court of law with divorce attorneys arguing over their assets. After that tiny confession, I doubted I'd be getting deluged with "best friend" applications. I know things do have a tendency to crash and break around me sometimes, but I promise—I cross my heart—I didn't have anything to do with all the marriage fallouts. If anything, I waged valiant one-woman campaigns for "sticking it out"—even when I was struggling in my own relationship.

The divorce of Couple Number One was by far the greatest shock. They were our best friends—the couple we'd sit around with, stay up late and talk with, and eat pizza out of a box on the coffee table with. They'd often have us over, along with other friends, to sing and strum guitars and eat chocolate chip cookie bars. And nearly always we'd tease about the ups and downs of being newly married. But we all knew we'd make it, for heaven's sake. We were Christians. And we all knew, for Christians especially, marriage is *forever,* and even if it wasn't the *greatest* at the *moment,* it would always get better around the next bend.

A couple of years went by, and we watched with joy as our friends became parents of a baby boy, and they loved that little guy so much.

Then, late one Sunday afternoon, we were visiting in their brand new home after supper. We all sipped coffee, laughed at their cute little guy playing in the corner, and oohed and ahhed over our newest baby boy sleeping in my arms. I looked up and smiled at our friends. She was leaning on his knee and his arm was around her shoulder.

"I think we're finally growing up," he announced, "We're going to make it." The evening sun cast a rosy glow through the window and onto the carpet, and all was well.

Two weeks later they were separated. He did not know there had been a lot of pain hiding behind her smile that Sunday afternoon. He tried to hide what had happened as long as he could from his "Christian" friends because Christians don't get divorced. When we found out, we phoned him right away.

"Come on over. Come now. You are our friend, our very best friend, and we love you. We'll order the pizza."

So he came, and none of us turned out to be very hungry after all. But our very best friend lay back on our couch and he talked and he cried and he hurt. And we talked with him and we cried with him and we hurt so bad that I thought all our hearts would break. He thanked us for still being his friend. We knew that no matter what happened next, we would always love this man. And though we were angry and confused, we knew we would always love her, too, for somewhere out there she was also hurting. Yes, the First Divorce was probably the hardest of all.

Amazingly, God has His own way of weaving broken threads into tapestries with the passage of time—tapestries made stronger and, in some ways, even more beautiful by the addition of those delicate, fragile, pain-filled strands. So it has been with our friends. A couple of years later our friend married a wonderful woman, and we loved her and unanimously adopted her right away. And now we get together and drink coffee, and talk 'til dawn, and eat pizza off boxes on dining room tables. And we are Best Couple Friends.

Couple Number Two's marriage died a slower, more predictable death. The wife had been friends with Scott since grade school—the proverbial girl next door. My husband has always had good taste in women, and I liked her immediately. Her husband was charming, with a deep voice and a wonderful sense of humor—but he almost never hugged his wife or told her he loved her. She was lonely almost as soon as they said, "I do." When she and I found ourselves pregnant at the same time, we became fast friends. The first time we got together for lunch, we ended up praying that God would heal what was wrong in her troubled marriage.

Housekeeping was never her forte. I love that in a person. And she smiled and laughed out loud a lot. Another ten points. I could tease her about always having only three things in the refrigerator to eat—bologna, Velveeta cheese, and red Kool-Aid—and she'd laugh it off as she asked if I wanted mayo or mustard on my bologna and cheese. I have to admit she could whip up a pretty mean sandwich and somehow it always tasted delicious at her house. Probably because she served it with lots of juicy talk and laughter—along with the bottomless glasses of Kool-Aid.

And then, her husband walked out. She was in agony, but she is a strong woman and her faith grew even stronger. After a few months she prayed him back home, and they had two happy years and one more child together. But then, he walked into the living room and told her she had gained too much weight from the last pregnancy and he couldn't find a clean sock. That was all he could take, and he walked out the door again—this time for good.

But this time she could not bring herself to pray for him to come back home, only to be hurt again. God gave her peace in letting him go. He married an old girlfriend soon after their divorce. And my girlfriend, well, she did what she always did best. She bloomed where she was planted. She made lemonade out of lemons. She smiled and laughed through her tears.

And even though a survey said it would be more likely to be killed by a terrorist than to marry after the age of thirty, she found a man. Not just any man. One who had never been married. One who was handsome and loved children and was involved in a good church and who had been waiting and praying for a woman who could laugh out loud and make great bologna and cheese sandwiches. God wove another tapestry out of yet another tangled mess.

In Couple Two, divorce had come through the door unwanted—and yet by the time it finally arrived, there was almost a sense of relief that the long, pain-filled cycle was over. I didn't hurt as badly or for as long as I did for the first couple, where I loved both parties equally and it all came as such a surprise.

But the Third Divorce has been a real doozey—for everyone, but especially for me. For one thing, I was a Marriage Counseling Graduate, and things were better for us, so I felt qualified to save my friends' marriages. For some time now Couple Number Three has appeared to be nicely on their way to Divorce Recovery. I, unfortunately, am still finding myself wiping away an occasional tear.

If you've read my past books, you might understand why this couple's breakup has been particularly tough for me. Number Three is so hard because it involved our good friends Gary and Mary. THE Mary of *Worms in My Tea,* the best friend/beauty operator that dyed my forehead purple and whose bright blue quote is blazoned on the back of our book announcing, "Becky, you have to find time to write a book, even if you do have the dirtiest floor in America."

And this divorce involved THE Gary of the Riding Lawnmower—the one who backed over the precious memorial sapling and went on to devour the screen door. Yes, and they are also one and the same Gary and Mary of the Window Story from this very book.

I'm so sorry to have to break the news like this, but Mary says I just can't go on writing about her and Gary as if they are married since they've been separated and/or divorced for nearly two years now—unless I'm going to start writing romantic *fiction,* that is.

I can almost joke about it now, but if ever there was a serious crusader out to save somebody else's marriage it was *moi*, with Gary and Mary as my projects. I just could not accept the fact that they couldn't work things out. Theirs appeared to be one of those easy-to-fix cases—no heinous sins, no knock-down-drag-outs. (Of course, marriage counselors say they'd rather work with angry, passionate couples than those who have no flame left to fan. Let's put it this way, Smokey the Bear would have been proud of Gary and Mary!)

I prayed and I empathized and consoled Mary for awhile, thinking this decision was a case of temporary insanity. When it came to actually signing the papers, I thought surely the shock of finality would bring them to their respective senses. Instead, their resolve to end the marriage grew more firm every day.

OK, I thought, *So you guys want to play hardball. Well, let's try some reason and common sense on for size.* I bought the book *Divorce Busting* and studied how to become a certified Divorce Buster Representative. I photocopied pages and memorized lines and even hand-delivered underlined copies of Top Ten Reasons Not to Go and Do a Stupid Thing Like Getting a Divorce for Pete's Sake for both parties to read at their leisure. Still no change.

As the court date drew near, I was getting more desperate. I thought about calling the governor to see if she could grant a stay in the execution of a good friend's marriage. Instead, I stopped by the church one summer afternoon, walked into the pastor's office, and made an announcement.

"Listen. This is getting serious. Gary and Mary think they are getting a divorce, and I'm sorry, but we just can't allow this to happen. I need heavy-duty prayer to stop it. So could you pray with me, please?" My pastor is a kind man. He graciously bowed his head and prayed with me. Though he probably knew I was up against something out of my control, I think he also knew that I was not yet ready to concede the possibility of defeat. Then I found two more ladies whom I felt were closer to God than I was, and I asked them to join me in a powerful where-two-or-more-are-gathered-together-in-My-name prayer.

The divorce date approached with unrelenting speed. There was no sign of letup. There was no alternative but to get tough. I finally lost it, yelling at Mary in frustration one night. Then I wrote her a long letter spelling out the scriptural error of her ways. I let her know I was putting into practice what I felt at the time was a painful, but necessary, last resort: I would be pulling away from our friendship altogether—hoping against hope that without my "enabling" support, she'd be struck by The Light, see the error of her ways, and ta-duumm, she and Gary would fall hopelessly in love with each other again and live happily ever after. God could make it happen. He hates divorce. He could do the impossible for my friends just as He had done the impossible for us. After all, didn't He see me wearing myself out to be His special little helper on this case?

For months, Mary and I stopped talking. On the day of her divorce, I did drive to her house, left her a Coke (we often brought each other Cokes for a treat) and a note telling her that I cared and I was sorry she was going through this day of pain and that I would always be her friend. But we were not on the same wavelength anymore. And we remained distant for many more months.

During that time, God began unraveling some important truths for me. First of all, I have no control over other people's lives. Some things are simply out of my hands. One day I was reading the biblical story of the paralytic. You know, the one where the friends cut a hole in the roof to give their buddy a chance to get close to Jesus, so that he might be healed. Suddenly, a phrase struck me right between the eyes. Luke wrote that the man's friends dropped him "right in front of Jesus" (Luke 5:19).

And I knew God was telling me, "Becky, that's what you must learn to do. Other people's problems are not yours to fix. You are a little Mothering Fixer-Upper by nature. But sometimes the only thing you can do for Mary, or anyone else for that matter, is give them to Me. Drop them right in front of Me. I'm the One who does the healing and I'll do it in My way, in My time. Remember?" So in my mind, I plunked Mary and Gary down the hole in the roof, right in front of Jesus. And amazingly, He's doing just fine with them, and all without my assistance.

Second, I realized that all that time I spent obsessing over Gary and Mary's breakup had drained my own family of energy. I was also neglecting other friends, so I redirected my focus toward reviving other friendships. I have to admit, angry as I was, I still missed Mary. She's always been amazingly accepting of me and my faults. I could tell her anything and know she'd never think less of me. She's forgiving. She's got a wonderful wit. She's a great conversationalist. She's the type of friend that's hard to replace. I missed a lot of things about being buddies.

Today, thanks to the Master Weaver, our friendship is on the mend, and I think it is even stronger for having gone through the fire. We are both still learning a lot, as individuals and as friends. For me, it's been about accepting the things I am powerless to change, about accepting people as they are, and then learning to extend a hand in grace rather than in judgment. It was painful for me to accept helplessness—the fact that there was nothing I could do to prevent one of my closest friends from taking a path that might lead her into even deeper pain. But Outcomes are God's department. And who am I to throw the first stone? We all fall short, all of us make messes of areas of our lives. We are all in need of grace.

Though Scott and I never made it to a divorce court, we both toyed with the idea. I've read countless articles on "How to Have a Marriage that Lasts Forever." Tucked into each one is usually a personal testimony about the mutual, steadfast avoiding of the word *divorce.* Testimonies like—

"Sure, we had our problems through the years, but we never, never, never uttered the word *divorce.* Murder, yes. Divorce, never. And that's why we've been able to stay happily married since dinosaurs roamed the earth."

I wish I could honestly say this was also true for us. I wish that the word *divorce* had never played dangerously about our heads or made its debut out of our mouths. I'm in wholehearted agreement with the theory that divorce is an escape hatch best left "off-limits." Unfortunately, we did tangle with the idea and got into some pretty major snarls as a result.

It was as if subconsciously we thought, *Well, if other couples that we know really well can get a divorce and survive, who's to say we wouldn't be better off?* Gradually, almost imperceptibly at first, that sort of thinking began to take seed. Then at times of great frustration, the seed burst forth and the possibility of divorce leaked into our thoughts and eventually burst out in the heat of anger. Once fired, the damage done was serious.

But in light of all of our frailties, I'd like to dedicate this chapter on the subject of divorce to anyone who has failed their marriage in any way. Whether you once failed in a marriage that is still alive and well today, or whether you failed in a marriage that did not survive the battle. Whether you were an initiator of the breakup, or whether you were the one who tried to hang on but just couldn't find a way to hold it together. Whether you have uttered the word *divorce* aloud, or just fantasized about it once or twice in the privacy of your own thoughts. Everyone I have ever talked with has messed up *big time* at some time in a relationship. So welcome to the human race.

There's one last thing I'd like to share before closing, with permission from an old friend. Remember the first wife of Couple Number One—the one that disappeared from our lives that beautiful Sunday afternoon? It had been fourteen years since we'd communicated. This year I found myself wishing I could reconnect personally with her—to put a sense of closure on old scars. So I wrote her a letter and I asked her to forgive me for not reaching out earlier. I told her that I still thought of her and cared about her. She wrote me back a book—twenty-six heartfelt pages. In part, here is what she had to say:

> Dear Becky,
>
> First let me say, to you and your precious family, including your mom and dad, how very sorry I am for any pain that I caused and for walking out with no explanation.
>
> Oh, guys, how I wish I could give you an explanation for our divorce—we both were lacking in communication skills and (as I learned in counseling right before I filed for divorce) missed each other's intentions and hearts for a long period of time. The vast chasm between us just seemed impossible to fill, especially since I did not believe that my God practically cared and could work in the situation. We were both *very* defensive and hurt, (could not hear each other) and I felt *so* alone. For some reason I could not accept myself because I could not handle the situation. I didn't trust others, and I hated myself—believing that I was defective and no one could help someone like me.
>
> Let me just say, divorce is not God's way, and I could never choose it again. I say that not on my own strength, but on the power of the Spirit who lives inside of me.
>
> Your conclusion that God can "take even the mistakes in our lives and weave them into a tapestry of beauty" is so true. I have married again—a wonderful man who is a friend, a companion, and the godly head of our home. Our son is growing tall and strong in the Lord, and we've been blessed with another daughter. He has led me through darkness and into His life and light, and I love Him for it.

And by the way, I now go by my middle name. I found out it means "One of Grace."

Her letter not only healed old scars; it was an incredible lift to my spirit. After all these years, God's grace has indeed made something beautiful out of all our weak and broken threads.

All in His way. All in His time.

When finally tangled webs we leave
Oh, what practiced Hands can weave!

BECKY FREEMAN © 1995

"For I'm going to do a brand new thing.
See, I have already begun!"

ISAIAH 43:19, TLB

FIFTEEN

Enjoy the local breakfasts and bed

Remember how I introduced this book? The part where I talked about wanting to share fragments of truth—ideas and actions—that have helped us improve our marriage? Well, it is now time to share one of the most significant fragments—a secret to unbridled bliss, if you will, that has revolutionized our relationship. A couple may increase their chances of experiencing this bliss—without any bridles whatsoever—by at least 78 percent if they will simply incorporate two suggestions (according to a recent galloping poll*). Actually, if these ideas really begin to catch on, we may eliminate divorce worldwide.

The big secret? Go out to breakfast together once or twice a week in a smoke-filled, bacon-sizzlin', small-town cafe. (Preferably, it should be located on a farm-to-market road next to a feed and ranch supply store.) And on at least one of those

* The 78 percent statistic was taken from a broad-based random survey based on my broad-based random imagination.

mornings it is important to go back home, while the kids are at school or at Mother's Day Out, and go back to bed together. And I don't mean to catch up on some "zzzz's." That's all there is to it. Busy couples just need to get away to a little more Breakfast and Bed.

Winston Churchill is said to have stated, "My wife and I tried two or three times in the last forty years to have breakfast together, but it was so disagreeable we had to stop."[1] Poor Winston. He should have come to me for advice first. He probably just did it all wrong. One has to follow important guidelines when breakfasting with a mate who is not, by nature, a morning person.

First, let's discuss the prerequisite of dining at old, cafe-type establishments. I know some of you big-city folk are already protesting. But I'm sorry; sharing a French croissant and sipping orange cappuccinos at La Madeliene's just won't cut the mustard if you are really serious about bliss. Drive an hour through traffic if you must, but get thee and thy betrothed unto the boonies. And don't stop until thou smellest pork on the grill and strong coffee at brew. If thou art greeted by a friendly, plain-faced waitress asking, "Whutkinah git you folks this mornin'?" thou hast surely uncovered a royal treasure.

Why *breakfast*, one may ask? What about meeting for a leisurely lunch or an elegant dinner? Those meals have particular lures of their own, I must agree, but I'm inclined to believe that mornings have special pressures of their own. And cooking a meal at that hour is way beyond the reaches of my imagination, however active it may appear.

Once I did offer to cook breakfast for my husband, but he would hear none of it. I had said, "Honey, I'm going to whip you up a little breakfast surprise with everything I have left in the refrigerator—Jimmy Dean sausage, fresh cranberries, and Actifed syrup." It took Scott no time at all to let me know that he wouldn't have his little woman slaving over a hot stove in the morning for all the cough syrup in China. Isn't he a prize?

But why insist on savoring this morning meal at a laid-back, old-fashioned *coffee shop?* Because in my opinion women do not need the added stress of having to doll themselves up before noon to go out to a fancy restaurant. Think about it, ladies. If you slip on a pair of faded jeans, a sweat shirt with a smiley face on it from 1974, tennis shoes with matching shoestrings, and slap on a bare smidgen of lipstick before walking through the door of a country cafe, I can almost guarantee you are going to be the most gorgeous woman in the joint. This is your chance to shine with the most minimal of effort.

Second, breakfast out in a simple cafe is an affordable habit. Even young couples on strict budgets can afford most items from the "Breakfast Specials." My personal favorite is homemade biscuits with gravy on the side for a mere buck fifty, or sometimes I'll go for a scrumptious breakfast burrito with hot sauce for a paltry ninety-five cents. Talk about a bargain. I always order a Coke *and* a cup of coffee because I like the taste of the Coke and the *smell* of the coffee. When meals are this cheap, you can afford to indulge in a few luxuries.

Another benefit you simply will not find in a la-de-da restaurant is what we country folk term *local color*. I mean, why pay for entertainment when it is sitting right there on a county road next to the feed and ranch supply store? As my dad says, "This is the kind of place where you can see some real characters."

My preference, as far as characters are concerned, is round tables full of lined-faced old-timers wearing overalls and baseball caps. Sometimes they wear wire-framed glasses, and they often have a chaw of tobacco tucked away in their front pocket. Like apparitions from days gone by, they have little on their morning agendas but sipping bottomless cups of coffee and shooting endless breezes.

In contrast, as soon as we are finished eating, Scott and I usually check our watches and discuss our busy schedules for the day. But many times, a quick glance over at the "What's Your

Hurry?" round table will make us think twice about getting up. By their mere presence, the old-timers make our bodies want to shift into slow gear. So quite often, we'll take a deep sigh instead, maybe even put our feet up on a nearby chair. It's a clincher that we are going to "set a spell" when Scott lifts his cup to the sweet-talking waitress and answers her standard inquiry with, "Sure. Fill 'er up one more time."

In my opinion, old-timers at coffee shops should be honored as the last genuine examples of American relaxation in a group setting. Once their generation is gone, we may never see it again. In this country-style, laid-back, coffee-serving atmosphere they help create, Cafe-Style Therapy begins to take place. Many a sore subject in our marriage has been successfully worked out over a checkered tablecloth in a wooden booth. And it's nearly impossible to get angry over controversial subjects when George Strait, Doug Stone, and Vince Gill are twanging out their ballads from a radio in the kitchen.

In this warm atmosphere, Scott and I are forced to talk in soft, pleasant tones to each other. As a result, we are almost always reluctant to end the conversation. A few times we've talked our way right through the breakfast bunch, past the mid-morning stragglers, and on into the time when the waitress writes the lunch specials on the chalkboard—all without realizing how much time has actually passed.

As I have stated plainly, I still do not like getting up early. But the idea of going out to eat will tantalize me out from under the covers most of the time. And the experience of having enjoyed a laid-back meal—of having had unhurried time with my husband—is usually enough to tantalize me back under the covers when we get home. This morning, as a matter of fact, Scott asked me if I wanted to come with him to get a bite of breakfast.

"Sure," I whispered sleepily. Then I added teasingly as I yawned and stretched, "And maybe then we can come back here for dessert."

Before taking off for the cafe, we still had to get the kids ready for school. As I was making up the bed in our bedroom, Gabriel poked his head around the corner. "Hey, Mom," he said, "how come Daddy's in such a good mood this morning?"

"What do you mean, Honey?"

"Well, he's whistling and singing and telling silly jokes out here in the kitchen."

"Hmmm," I answered, "I think he's just excited about getting to go out to breakfast with li'l ol' me, Sugar Pie."

Scott rounded the corner just in time to hear my explanation and then gave me an exaggerated wink along with a grin that melted me like—like butter on a stack of fresh hotcakes.

So there you have it—the quick and easy secret to continued marital bliss: Linger for breakfast at an old-time cafe and give your partner a round-trip ticket back home for dessert. If only these mom-and-pop restaurants would stay open on stress-producing holidays, Scott and I might remain in a state of married bliss from here to eternity.

If an outing to the local Breakfast and Bed is not your cup of java, I hope you will find a way to spend some time alone together on a regular basis doing something you both are crazy about doing. Particularly in the years of raising a family, it's the best system I know for "romancing the home."

Go, eat your food with gladness, and drink . . . with a joyful heart. . . . Enjoy life with your wife, whom you love.

ECCLESIASTES 9:7, 9

SIXTEEN

"Good mornin', Mary Sunshine! Please go back to bed"

I realize by this point that I've spent a good deal of time sharing the unusual penchant Scott and I have for long, meaningful, uplifting conversations. You are entitled to ask, "But exactly what sort of things are said in those intriguing little chats?" So I thought it might be well to invite you to eavesdrop on an actual conversation with my husband that started last night and continued upon rising this morning—sort of a real-life example of how effective communication takes place in a home.

Please keep in mind that Scott is a natural born philosopher. I've even begun to think of our small lake as my husband's own Walden Pond. Most of the time it is here that he works and walks and weaves his intriguing form of logic for the entertainment of family and passersby.

Last night I was in the kitchen when I overheard Scott discuss a news item with Zach and Zeke, who as teenagers are recognizing that the world they inhabit can be hard to figure out at times. A tragedy had occurred in a nearby town—apparently a pastor had killed his wife and then had taken his own life by jumping from a bridge.

"Dad," Zeke asked, "what made him *do* that?"

I braced for Scott's answer, hoping against hope he might say something like, "Well, Son, we just don't know. But there are a few people in this world who just snap under pressure."

But no, he looked my impressionable son straight in the eye and said, "Boys, it's time you realized that everybody's crazy."

Now, I'm delighted that Zach and Zeke adore their father, but I don't want them to get the wild idea that every person they see, including themselves, are candidates for the funny farm. So I jumped into the conversation and begged to differ.

"Scott, not *everybody* is crazy. That's ridiculous."

"*You* are crazy."

"I know, but that's not the point. The *whole human race* isn't crazy."

"Yes it is."

"Where do you get that idea?"

"Romans 3:23 says that 'All have sinned and fall short of the glory of God.'"

"Your point?"

"That means everybody's crazy. Some people *do* accept God's grace. But, even so, we're still all crazy as Betsy Bugs." I decided to drop the conversation before I turned the wooden spoon I was holding into a lethal weapon or got the urge to go jump off a bridge myself.

That night, Scott turned in early, but I stayed up late reading and writing. Young mothers are always faced with the dilemma: How can I possibly go to bed and waste all this peaceful solitude *sleeping?!* So by the time I crawled into bed, I glanced at the clock and saw it beamed 2:00 A.M. through the darkness. *I might be dead on my feet all day tomorrow,* I thought to myself, *but it was worth it!*

Seconds later it seemed, some large, male lunatic woke me up by throwing the covers off my snuggled-up body. "Get up,

Miss Peeky" he shouted cheerfully (Scott likes to call me that). "Get up!" He hovered over my face, bouncing on the bed like a friendly puppy while my heart struggled to get up to a semblance of a regular beat. "Your daughter needs you to make her an egg!"

It is a burden to be married to a Morning Person.

"She knows how to make an egg!" I hollered back. "And my name is not Miss Peeky! And don't wake me up like that again, either. It's rude and unthoughtful and that light's giving me a headache!"

Undaunted, Scott smiled happily and began to chant, "Peek-y is crank-y, Peek-y is crank-y."

For the sake of my children, I managed to pull myself out of the bed and into an upright position. Opening my eyes was not an option at the moment, but I felt my way toward the kitchen where a distinct sulfurous odor filled the air. Following the smell and heat, I found Rachel pouring what looked like little yellow erasers into a bowl. I managed to bring one corner of my mouth up and into a semi-smile and lean against the oven. With this support, I found the strength to offer my assistance.

"Do you need help, Honey? Those scrambled eggs look a little tough."

"No," Rachel answered brightly, "I'm doing fine. And by the way, that's a fried egg."

I've trained my children well. Where food is concerned, they have very low expectations and will eat just about anything edible served at any degree of doneness.

I turned my attention to Zeke. "Zeekle, Honey, do you want me to help you with your eggs?"

He gave me the once-over and in his new boy/man voice ordered, "Mom, go sit down on the couch. I cook my own eggs all the time."

At that moment Scott came whistling out of the shower, wrapped in a towel. He walked over to the couch where I was still trying to pry open one eyelid with my fingers and planted a kiss on my cheek.

"See how nice it is when you get up and help the children?" he said merrily. "Why don't *you* drive them to the bus stop today?"

Oh, please, not that. No, no, no. That would mean I would have to put on a pair of pants and get both legs in the right holes too! But Scott was determined that I needed to do this. When all the kids were loaded into the station wagon and had nearly strangled each other over frontseat privileges, I collapsed into the driver's seat and started the engine. Mr. Morning Man was now watering the flowers in the front yard and playfully squirting my car window with the hose. He waved at me with a silly grin plastered on his face until I was completely out of the driveway. I thought grimly to myself, *He looks like Laurel from one of those old Laurel and Hardy movies.*

The second I reached the stop sign, all the kids piled out and headed across the street to wait for the bus. Though I was still fighting fatigue, I remembered to wave at them and even blew kisses in their direction from across the road where I was parked. Suddenly Rachel stopped, turned, and jogged back across the street to tell me something. *Isn't that sweet?* I thought. *She probably wants to tell me she loves me and enjoyed my getting up with her this morning.* Instead, my daughter began pleading with me through the side window.

"Please *go away*, Mother. The bus is almost here and the kids might see you." I glanced in the mirror at my uncombed hair and unmade face and immediately saw her point.

When I pulled into the driveway back home, Scott was no longer in sight. I walked to the front door and leaned against it hoping against hope someone with the strength to open it would happen along. In a few seconds, Scott opened the door and I fell into his arms. He responded to me in precisely the way I would have hoped, probably because I was comatose and noncombative. He patted my back and spoke soothingly.

"Poooooor Peeeeky," he crooned. "You have such a hard time with morning. I'll tell you what. I'll do most of the mornings from now on. It'll be my special time with the kids. My contribution to the family."

Did I say my husband looked like Laurel? No, no, I meant he looked like an incredibly handsome Hercules with the Nobel-prize winning compassion of Mother Teresa. As he led me to a chair and brought me a cup of coffee, I wept in gratitude all over his shirt sleeve.

He wanted to renew our theological discussion from the night before. He seems to especially enjoy morning conversations with me. I think it's because he knows he has an unfair advantage. He talked of all of the people in the Bible who God had used even though they had "messed up real bad." This was to substantiate last evening's point that everybody's crazy. I might have been down for the count, but I was not totally out. With what strength I could muster, I raised my head from the kitchen counter.

"Not Joseph," I manage to squeak. "Joseph always did the right thing. And Daniel too."

Scott laughed and pinched my cheeks. "You're so cute." Then he imitated my squeaky voice—"Not Joseph. And *not* my Daddy!"

I ignored his teasing and, gathering more strength, sat up on the bar stool to my full height. "That's right. And not my kids. *They* won't mess up and be crazy."

He grinned and poured himself another cup of coffee. "Becky, we work well together. You think our children are going to be perfect, and I think they're going to mess up. Either way, they've got a parent who believes in them."

This is a weird way to raise kids, I mused, and slumped back to my head-on-the-counter position. Scott interrupted my thoughts by slamming his hand on the counter, bringing me upright once again.

"Oh, shoot!" he moaned. "We missed Earl Pitt's radio spot! He's starting a 'Save the Ugly Vegetable Society.' He's all up in arms about hard-hearted vegetarians cutting the eyes out of innocent potatoes and brutally chopping off the heads of cabbages."

This is the sort of deep, meaningful conversation we are capable of having before 8:00 A.M.—one topic always flowing smoothly into the next. I was reminded of George Eliot's immortal words: "O, the comfort, the inexpressible comfort of feeling safe with a person, having neither to weigh thoughts nor measure words, but pouring them all right out just as they are, chaff and grain together."[1]

This conversation was classic chaff, but it was cozy in a way, this mindless chitchat. So many women complain, "My husband never talks to me!" So I consider myself lucky. But even so, it was apparent that someone needed to throw a little "grain" into the mixture of this chitchat and see if it couldn't be raised to a little higher level. So I took the bull by the horns and changed the subject to one of deeper significance. I told Scott about the Oprah Winfrey show I had seen the day before.

It was a "Sleepless in Seattle" episode where they matched a widower with a date. I told him how much the widowers missed their first wives and how much they had loved each other and how you never knew when one of us could be gone. The enormity of it hit me, and I wiped a tear from my eye. Scott came over to my chair, leaned down, and kissed me passionately. (That is really love considering the way I looked and the fact that my teeth hadn't yet encountered a toothbrush.) Then he said something else that was odd but, in its own way, touching.

"Peeky," he said, "for somebody I can't stand, I certainly am crazy about you." My eyes gazed deeply into his.

"I know," I replied in earnest. "I feel exactly the same way about you." Then I asked him the same question I ask him nearly every day. It's almost become a ritual.

"We love each other so much, don't we?" He answered as he always does.

"Yes, we love each other so much." Just before Scott left for work, he tossed me one last bit of philosophical cud to chew. "What we have got here, Becky, is a dioclassical relationship."

I blinked at that one, but it was like him. He's always inventing words. When we were courting he would take me on nature walks and pretend to be some sort of naturalist—making up scientific-sounding names for the plant life along the trail. They sounded so authentic and believable that I was actually fooled for a while. I believe it was the "paleoedible chlorophillia endometriosis" that finally clued me in.

Scott bulldozes his way through the minefield of psychology and its jargon in much the same way. Standing in the doorway, he expounded one last word on his new theory before bidding me farewell.

"A dioclassical relationship is one in which two people who are totally opposite—who irritate each other constantly—each grow to find the other completely irresistible."

With that explanation, he gave me a quick good-bye kiss and darted out the front door. I glanced sleepily at the clock. I was due for a radio interview in half an hour to publicize *Worms in My Tea,* and I realized I must somehow get coherent. I couldn't remember where the broadcast was from, but I hoped it was from the city of Seattle. I wondered how the Sleepless in Seattle people would feel about an interview with Tired in Texas. I'd like to tell those heartbroken widowers and widows not to be too particular about marrying the perfect mate next time around. After all, there's even love to be found for two dioclassical crazy people. As long as they master the art of effective, meaningful communication.

And he informed me, and talked with me, and said . . .
"I have now come forth to give you skill to understand. . . .
for you are greatly beloved."

DANIEL 9:22–23, NKJV

SEVENTEEN

Advice from a pro

This past September I opened my mailbox and found an envelope. It had a fragile appearance, the edges slightly yellowed. The letter inside had obviously been typed on an old manual typewriter, deepening my impression that I was holding something timeless and special in my hand. The return address read "A. Gordon" of Savannah, Georgia.

Arthur Gordon had written a book, *A Touch of Wonder,* over twenty years ago. It has turned out to be one of my all-time favorites. The title caught my eye as I was browsing in an offbeat bookstore, and it was one of those books that came to me at just the right moment to fill just the right spot. His affirmative way of viewing life lifted my spirits when the going was tough. It also made me doubly thankful when the going was good.

Since I had been so moved by his book, I determined to find him and tell him so in a letter.

Even though Mr. Gordon had written more than ninety articles for *Reader's Digest,* no one I talked to at the magazine had heard from him since 1988. However, I eventually located an editor at *Guideposts* magazine who agreed to steer my letter to the proper hands. While waiting for a reply, I dug for more interesting tidbits about Mr. Gordon and his life.

I discovered Arthur Gordon has intriguing Southern roots. He hails from Savannah, Georgia, and is the nephew of Juliette Gordon Low, world-famous founder of Girl Scouts. The memories he records of his feisty aunt are priceless. He was educated at Yale and then went on to Oxford as a Rhodes scholar. He fought in the United States Air Force as a lieutenant colonel during the Second World War, receiving both the Air Medal and the Legion of Merit.

But to me, one of the most interesting of Gordon's experiences was the day he spent in the little village of Burwash, England, with Rudyard Kipling. Yes, *the* Rudyard Kipling—author of *The Jungle Book* and the immortal collection of *Just So Stories.* Mr. Gordon was a young man just starting his career; Kipling was sixty-nine and in ill health. Gordon had been offered a secure teaching job back home in America, but his dream was to become a writer. He hoped this meeting with Kipling, one of the world's greatest writers, might provide some direction for his own life's work. The two men ended up talking at length while sitting in a boat in the middle of a fish pond. So deep were they in conversation that Gordon never got around to asking for that direction, but without his asking, and in the course of conversation, he received his answer.

"Do the things you really want to do," Kipling told him. "Don't wait for circumstances to be exactly right. You'll find that they never are."[1]

With those words ringing in his head, young Mr. Gordon went home to America, turned down the teaching post, and got to work on his dream of writing. And one day that young man would go on to write a book about Wonder.

"Lord of all things," it begins, "whose wondrous gifts to man include the shining symbols knowns as words, grant that I may use their mighty power only for good."

Today that man is in the winter of his life. And I, fairly new at this business of crafting "shining symbols," am finding encouragement and example in the words he wrote many years ago.

In my letter to him I had asked, gingerly, a personal favor. Would he share some personal reflections for those whose marriages might be going through "a rough patch," as the British say? He graciously answered my request in the letter condensed below.

Dear Becky,

Many thanks for your nice note and the kind words about ATOW. If you're a writer yourself, you know that admiration is the fuel we run on. So an unexpected gallon or so does help.

Marriages in trouble. I have noticed that when the going gets really rough the partners tend to demonize each other, see nothing good, only the bad. Result is, mutual appreciation dies and there's nothing to cushion the shock in quarrels or recriminations. If the combattants would make an effort to recall one or two things they used to admire in their partner and force themselves to say so, however grudgingly, it might save the marriage. See the last sentence or two in the chapter in ATOW called "How Wonderful You Are." Maybe you can make something of all this.

How many t's in combatant, I wonder. One is probably enough.

Good luck with your new book project. I envy you your energy!

Best regards,

AG

Smiling, I made myself a cup of gourmet coffee and returned to my chair, this time with my dog-eared copy of *A Touch of Wonder.* I opened the chapter Mr. Gordon had mentioned and remembered at once it had been a favorite.

"To be manifestly loved," I had underlined, "to be openly admired are human needs as basic as breathing. Why, then, wanting them so much ourselves, do we deny them so often to others? Why indeed?"

Great question, an answer for which I am still mute. There is no reason, with any solid legs to stand on, for human beings to withhold their admiration from each other. After all, it isn't as if by hoarding our words of praise we are keeping anything of value for ourselves.

At that point, I made an important decision—one I'd been contemplating for some time. I would do all I could do in my remaining years to focus on the *best*—not only in my husband, but in all of life. And when I came across something wonderful—especially in my loved ones—I determined to openly share my admiration.

Do not withhold good from those who deserve it, when it is in your power to act.

Proverbs 3:27

EIGHTEEN

Looking for gold with rose-colored glasses

Perhaps a pair of rose-colored glasses should be issued to couples a year after the honeymoon as a reminder to accentuate the positive.

Gary Paulsen is a sensitive, award-winning writer of young adult fiction. In his book *Clabbered Dirt, Sweet Grass* he compares the grain pouring out of a threshing machine to gold: "Rich, pouring, a river of gold as grand as the cream that comes from the separator is the wheat or barley or oats, and the dust and noise and itching and red eyes are forgotten in that river of richness."[1]

In an interview with *Writer's Digest* magazine in July of 1994, Gary Paulsen comments on this use of "perception" as a writer's device, but as I read his comments I saw a much broader application. He used life on the farm as an example.

> If you turn it just slightly, a lot of the stuff on the farm would be ugly. But if you dwelled on that and looked at it from that angle, it would ruin the book, the beauty that you're trying to see. So what you do is you hold up each thing and you say,

> I wish to write about working with the threshing machine and threshing grain—which I've done and know how hard it is, and I know the dangers of it, with that *?!#! belt humming right next to your face. But if I wrote that sense of it, it would change what I was trying to say. And so I looked for the beauty in the wheat: the gold coming out of the threshing machine, that rich grain that just runs and is the most incredible thing. I chose the perception, the view I took of the diamond . . . . I just decided from what angle to look at them.[2]

The correlation is painfully obvious, is it not? The lazy, obvious way to view others is to focus on the "threshing machine belts" in their personalities. Unfortunately it doesn't take long, at this angle, to "demonize" the loved ones we used to admire—as Mr. Gordon's letter had warned. It takes a conscious decision to "choose the perception," perhaps even squinting at times, to see the gold in those we love. And if we, as husbands and wives, could find a way to do that consistently, I'm convinced we'd wind up with a marriage that "just runs and is the most incredible thing." Such small determinations, such vital differences. A small rudder turns 'round an enormous ship.

As to changing one's point of view, some of the best advice I've heard for couples who are stuck in a miserable cycle is this: Stop It. Fix It. Do It Now.

If a good marriage is something we really "want to do," we can't wait around for better times, more money, less stress, or the other person to change. We've got to determine now, today, *we* are going to go for the gold.

And so it is with all of life, really. A few years ago, I realized it only *made sense* to concentrate on the good—the river of gold—whenever I had a choice in the matter. After all, the negative pushes its way into our lives like an annoying houseguest—every day. But the positives—like gold—take more effort to glean. I determined to do whatever it takes to make the changes in myself that could lead to a rocking-chair-love-affair marriage.

Thankfully along the way, Scott independently came to a similar conclusion. Knowing now that I am helpless to control another human being, I am supremely thankful that Scott has chosen "us." And not just "us," but he wants the best possible, growing-old-happy-together "us" too. My husband has made it perfectly clear that he is in this relationship for the long haul. Good times and bad. Sickness and health. Holidays and Blah Days. Crazy About Each Other and Ready to Strangle One Another. Commitment is a *gift,* freely given—one I could never demand, but one I cherish as no other.

Also out of that turning point—that realization that the "gold" in life is worth the effort to find—came a poem summing up my Philosophy of Life. On the days when my life lines up with the words of this poem, I find a tremendous peace and sense of good.

No, I Won't Take Off My Rose-Colored Glasses

It only makes sense to fill my mind with the Goodness of God
to leave the hard questions in His Hand
to trust He sees the Big Picture, when I don't

To fill my ears with music that soars—and honors love

To fill my mind with Scripture, great books, vivid poetry—
courageous, joyful, dancing words

To fill my eyes with the smiles of children,
and watercolor sunsets

To fill my senses with the sound of my Love's voice,
and the touch of his skin

To spend time with those who have been seasoned
with warmth and wisdom—who've walked a long time with
the Friend of Friends

To fill these walls with laughter splashing over,
so that our home beckons, "Come and join!"

If I don't, the World will surely fill the empty spaces in my head
With unrelenting news of violence, hate and destruction—
and when I'm worn to the ground in Despair
how can I help those who need me most?
If my cup is not full of Light—
What will I have to share
with those who cry out in their Darkness?

No, I won't take off these Rose-Colored Glasses,
I work too hard to keep them on

Becky Freeman © 1994

It is amazing how much better life looks with some rose-colored shades. Gold begins popping up all over the place.

To be held in living esteem is better than gold.

Proverbs 22:1, TLB

N I N E T E E N

Holidays on ice

I love this day. It is the third day of January, my sister Rachel's birthday. Come to think of it, I believe it's her big "3-0." While this is great cause for celebration, I must admit, there is an even greater one. In addition to being Rachel's birthday, today is also the most thrilling of all the holidays for millions of stay-at-home moms. It is the day *after* Christmas vacation—the day kids go back to school and husbands go back to work. This is the day life gets back to normal. Yes, I *love* this day.

My poor children, however, looked as if they were marching off to the guillotine when I rounded them up for the school-bound carpool. I hoped they wouldn't notice the spring in my own step, so uncharacteristic of me at an early hour. Scott was faring no better than the kids. He looked at me with sad, puppy-dog eyes.

"Which tie looks best on me," he asked, "in case I decide to hang myself with it instead of facing rush-hour traffic again?"

I gave him my best sympathetic hug, but I had to work hard at suppressing the smile twitching at the corners of my lips. I couldn't help it—this was to be the first day in weeks that I would find myself alone—*alone at last!!!* My feeble attempt to control my excitement faltered as Scott apparently read my mind. He walked out the front door and turned for a parting shot.

"It seems to me the *least* you could do is quit humming the 'Hallelujah Chorus' under your breath."

For some years now, I have fought the creeping awareness that the holidays make the old, everyday variety of stress seem like a trip to the beach. For me, taking down the Christmas tree and the festive feeling that goes with it far exceeds the "sounding joy" of putting it up. Scott and I are finally ready to admit that we are hopelessly holiday impaired. If there is a twelve-step program for cranky-on-special-occasion-aholics, please let me know. We are at the end of our merry ropes.

I would have preferred to write this chapter as if I were looking in on some past problem that we used to have and could report that now everything is just peachy at our house from Thanksgiving through New Year's Day. But this particular area of our marriage remains a giant puzzle. We simply don't handle holidays well. Or any special occasion. And the hitch is, holidays seem to appear every year with relentless regularity.

It is hard to confess this because so much joy and warmth and *specialness* is supposed to begin bubbling up around Thanksgiving, Christmas, Valentine's, and other days of that ilk. Unfortunately for us, Groundhog Day, St. Patrick's Day, and—for heaven's sake—even Daylight Saving's Day can cause Scott and me to evolve into walking nervous ticks. You name the holiday, we've blown it to smithereens.

In our first year of marriage, Scott was such a bundle of nerves about his newlywed Valentine's Day performance that he signed his romantic card to me using his first *and* last name. It read, "To my darling Sweetheart. I will always love you. Sincerely, Scott Freeman."

Ironically, we are fairly jolly souls on regular days. We only turn into jerks on days when we are *expected* to be jolly. The added pressure pushes us over the edge when it is imperative for all to be calm and all to be bright.

So it should have been no surprise that this year—like most years—Scott and I found ourselves fighting to keep the Grinch within from stealing Christmas from all of us. Occasionally, we actually won the battle. But far too often we let the Grinches and the Scrooges in our personalities have the upper hand. It didn't help that I began this Christmas vacation with my stress level already set at low simmer. Even as I was writing a chapter for this book, it became painfully obvious that I was suffering from a severe case of burnout. How did I come to this revelation? Let me back up to the Monday before school let out for the holidays.

As I was trying to decide whether to go Christmas shopping, put up a tree, write Christmas cards, finish my chapter, clean the house, get dressed, or bake goodies for the kids' class parties, the phone rang. It was the principal of the kids' school.

"Mrs. Freeman," she said in a clipped voice, "could you come in today? There is something I'd like you to see."

"I'll be there in fifteen minutes," I answered before grabbing my purse and heading out the door. I had a strange feeling that the something she'd like me to see was going to be something I didn't particularly *want* to see. But if I had to see something I didn't want to see today, I wanted to get it over with as soon as possible.

I arrived at the school and walked down the hall toward the office. At one point I had to step over two school backpacks lying on the floor. Numerous papers had obviously made their way out of the backpacks and onto the surrounding floor. As I stepped over them to reach the office doors I thought, *Somebody ought to pick this stuff up. This sort of mess could be a real safety hazard.*

I walked into the office and was immediately greeted by the well-groomed and equally well-tailored principal. We shook hands and exchanged pleasantries as she steered me out of the office and back toward the spot where the two backpacks lay unfurled. On second examination, I realized the backpacks looked rather familiar. As a matter of fact, I was beginning to believe they might be the ones belonging to my two oldest sons. The principal got right to the point.

"Do you recognize these bags, Mrs. Freeman?"

"Should I have an attorney present before I answer that question?"

"No. Actually, I know to whom they belong. But do you know *why* they are here?"

"No." I was running out of clever responses.

"Well, they are here because out of the *entire* elementary school, there were only *two children* who had to dump their backpacks in order to find their permission slips for the field trip today. Would you like to guess who those two children were?"

I shook my head in the negative, but that didn't stop her from telling me.

"Zach and Zeke have had *two weeks* to get their permission slips turned in, so it is not as if we sprang this on them yesterday."

"But I signed those slips a week ago!" I protested. At this point, her control was beginning to slide and her eyes had a mild look of hysteria to them.

"Oh, no doubt. But your boys forgot to turn them *in!* So this morning, while an entire busload of students waited to depart for "The Nutcracker," your sons sat cross-legged in this hall, frantically searching their backpacks for their permission slips! Luckily, they found them. If they had not, I assure you they would not be seeing the ballet today."

"I'm so sorry. They do seem to have trouble getting organized."

Gathering her remaining wits about her, the principal continued in a more professional tone of voice. "Well, I am going to have to ask you to help them get a grip on this thing over the holiday break. They are the sweetest boys, but if you could see the insides of their desks you wouldn't believe it."

"Oh, I might. But I guess I am partly to blame. I've always had a problem getting my act together too."

We talked a few more minutes. But just as I was pledging to be more diligent about helping the boys get ordered, I happened to glance at my reflection in the office window. Even in the faint outline of the glass, it was easy to see that something was bobbing atop my head. *What is that?* I thought. Reaching up, I pulled one bright pink curler out of my bangs. I smiled up weakly at the principal.

Slowly, desperately, she shook her head as if to say, "What's the use?"

Weakened in spirit from being called to the principal's office, I eventually experienced that horrible phenomenon commonly referred to as Writer's Block. It is not subtle either, this infamous Writer's Block. It lands upon its victims' heads with a resounding thud. The first indication something was awry came to me as I was rereading the opening I had written for a new chapter.

> So here we are in the middle of this book. Ta-duuuummmm!
>
> I'd sure like some fudge. With lots of nuts.
>
> I wonder why they make those Styrofoam packing thingies look like big white peanuts?
>
> The End.

At that point I should have turned off the computer, put on an apron, and whipped up batches of burnt cookies. That always seems to lift my spirits. You know, the fragrance in the air, the joyous buzzing of the smoke alarm. But this time, I was beyond a quick sugar-and-smoke-alarm fix. Instead, I took to bed and made a list of fifteen people whom I felt I had disappointed or let down in some way. I do not recommend this as a Christmas tradition. I cried for the better part of the day, and thus primed the pump to respond at the slightest provocation for the rest of the season.

My daughter, Rachel, the one who is sometimes gifted with a heavenly wisdom beyond her years, crawled into bed with me and put her arms around me.

"Momma," she said matter-of-factly, "you can cry today all you want to and you can feel sorry for yourself for just *today*. But tomorrow you have to knock it off and get up and put some makeup on. Because to tell the truth, you look like roadkill."

I graciously accepted her offer and hosted the most pitiful of semi-private pity parties known to women. For one day only, I promised her and myself. OK, I must admit there was quite a bit of residual sniffing still going on the next day. But at least I managed to get my sad self out of bed the next morning.

At first Scott tried to play the comforter. That role doesn't suit my husband longer than about three hours. It wasn't long before his "sympathizer batteries" ran out and he said something snippy to me and I said something ugly back to him and then he shouted at me.

"How could you act like this during Christmas vacation?"

"How can *you* be so insensitive during the most holy of holidays?" I railed back at him.

A couple of days later we were still, shall we say, not up to par. But we loaded the kids in the station wagon anyway and set off for my parents' house to celebrate an Arnold Christmas—one week early. Mother and Daddy would be going to Virginia to spend Christmas with my sister, Rachel, and her little family, so we had planned an early family celebration.

On the way there, the engine on our panel wagon must have picked up on the mood inside the car, and it began to overheat. We pulled over and parked under a bridge where Scott used a bottle he found on the ground to scoop up questionable looking water from nearby puddles to pour on the steaming radiator. The kids were fascinated by the bottle, and I told them I thought this would be a really good time to play the Quiet Game. Through my open window, I could hear Scott muttering to himself.

"Is it not humiliating enough to be the only couple driving a station wagon with wood-grain panels on the sides? Oh, no! Now strangers are getting a chance to see me and my family parked under a bridge while I forage for used bottles."

He was finally able to resuscitate the car and coax it back home where we reloaded the six of us into Scott's mini-pickup truck. By the time we reached my parent's house, I walked through their front door a few steps behind the kids, smiled a big plastic smile, and bravely said, "Merry Chriswaaahhhh!. . ." Then for the first time in years, I collapsed sobbing into my mother's arms.

Mother swept me into a back bedroom and into the hug I needed.

"Honey," she said as she handed me a Kleenex, "I've been wondering when this was going to happen."

"You have?" I asked, gulping back tears. I had fancied myself a strong and independent woman, but here I was at my mommie's house, blubbering like a child again. I hated losing control, but at the same time—after all that had been building up inside—it was a relief to let it all out. I spewed and sputtered like our overheated car for several minutes. When I finally began to cool down, Mother gently unstuck my hair from the side of my teary face and pushed it back so we could see each other. She looked like she was underwater.

"Look at what you've taken on this year, Honey. Our first book has only been out a few months with a second one due out this spring, and you're already writing a third one on your own! And every time I talk to you, you've got new ideas for other projects that keep your mind going on constant fast forward. On top of that, this is the first year you've started to speak in public. Add financial stress to this new 'career' and a marriage that you value, four kids who need you, housekeeping duties, cherished relationships to keep up with . . . "

"And I'm blowing it in every category, Mother," I wailed. "What am I going to do?"

"For starters, you need a break. *Nobody* can do it all! A lot of the pressure you're feeling may be coming from your own mind. Recently I discovered something about myself that surprised me. I am, in many ways, a perfectionist. I care so much about what other people think of me that the stress of wanting to please had started to effect me physically." She paused, and I thought, *Gee, even fifty-something, mature women deal with this?*

"I also think," she continued, "that everybody talks to themselves in one way or another, all day long, and sometimes that self-talk can turn into self-condemnation. Lots of times we think others are upset with us when they really aren't. I'm having to learn to retrain my thoughts. I read somewhere that the "default mode" of the human mind is negative. It comes naturally. So we have to purposely direct our minds to think positive thoughts about ourselves, and about others. That only comes supernaturally."

"But, Mother! I'm giving speeches on how to have wonder and joy in life! With all I know to be true, why am I so down right now?"

"Because you need to hear someone tell you the same things you tell others. We all need to hear a genuine human being say to us personally, 'Be kind to yourself.' Becky, you're exhausted. You've just overdone it. Take it easy and be gentle with yourself for awhile. Let the Lord show you what really is essential and how to do it."

When the chips are down, my mother knows how to give comfort like no one else I've ever known. As she has admitted to herself, she isn't perfect. But even when I was a child, I always thought her ability to empathize was a special gift. Her mother before her, my Nonnie, had the same uncanny knack for knowing exactly what to say to soothe frazzled minds.

In those few minutes, bathed in the warmth of my mother's understanding and compassion, I began to feel life and strength slowly flowing back into my wilted mind and body. My thoughts turned to Christ, who left His peaceful home to "beam down" to our world—to have His fresh-born senses invaded by noise and rush and aches and pains. But somehow He knew the secret of keeping The Peace—be it in a noisy animal stall, a storm-tossed boat, or in the midst of pressing crowds on special holidays.

Like the shepherds and wise men of old, I was suddenly filled with a sense of urgency. I wanted to gather up my family and go find this Christ Child, this Prince of Peace. Wouldn't it be lovely to simply be still and worship quietly, for even a few moments, at His side?

Scott and I had one week before the Real Christmas Day to find out if the holiday impaired might begin the process of becoming holy repaired.

"Come to me, all you who are weary and burdened,
and I will give you rest.
Take my yoke upon you and learn from me,
for I am gentle and humble in heart,
and you will find rest for your souls.
For my yoke is easy and my burden is light."

MATTHEW 11:28–30

T W E N T Y

Scott finally quacks up

I turned over in bed one morning a couple of days before December 25th, opened one sleepy eye, and glanced at my husband snoring happily on his pillow beside me. Something was different about him. I opened my eyes wider and moved closer for another look.

Then I reached toward Scott's face thinking, *Is that thing what I think it is?* It was. For some odd reason my husband's upper lip had ballooned during the night and now completely draped over his bottom lip. I was on the emotional mend, but apparently the holiday stress had begun to have a most unusual effect on him.

"Wake up, Scott!" I shouted. "I think you're turning into a duck!"

As you can well imagine, Scott sat as straight up in the bed as he could, considering the added weight of his lip, and gingerly patted it. Dropping it over the side of the bed, he looked into the mirror at what appeared to be a large, fleshy beak. Then she turned pitifully back to me.

"It's finawy happened," he managed to say. "I'm awergic to Chwistmas. And pwobabwy my wife too." He sat staring into space trying to adjust to new realities for another minute or two, and then his morbid gaze happened to fall upon a book I had just purchased on the subject of joy. He grabbed the paperback and stared at me, his eyes tormented with suspicion. The title? *Talking to Ducks*.

We made it through the morning, and at noon I offered to fix him some soup, but he said he wasn't sure he could get a spoon through his lips.

"Oh, come on, Honey," I coaxed. "Try to eat a little. It'll be duck soup." I flopped on the bed with convulsions of laughter. He didn't seem to find that helpful.

We never found out exactly what had caused his deformity, but we were enormously grateful it turned out to be temporary. After that crisis had subsided, we were faced with yet another problem. For the first time, Scott and I would be spending Christmas Eve at home with just the six of us. We've always spent Christmas Eve with Grannie Ruthie and PawPaw George or Grandma and Grandpa Freeman where we were aided in bringing good cheer by a number of cousins. From the moment we dropped the Home Alone bomb, our kids were nervous wrecks.

It was a painful struggle for them—wrestling with the whole concept of trusting *us,* their own parents, with the enormity of staging Christmas Eve. I did realize that my children hated the artificial—but authentic-looking—Christmas tree I put up every year. And sure, I've accidentally burned the arms and legs off more than my share of gingerbread men. But it was truly a blow to our egos to realize that our children didn't believe their mother and father had the maturity, or wherewithal, to conduct a major holiday event without more responsible adult supervision around.

We set out to prove them wrong. We'd show them we could handle a family holiday with the biggest and best of grown-ups. I'd turned over a new leaf last week at Mother's. We'd do something rich with sentiment, a time they would never forget. We'd take them to the mall.

This was not just any mall. This was the Galleria Mall in downtown Dallas, where there was skating, huge Christmas trees, caroling in the background, gorgeous decorations, and hot cappuccinos beckoning from sidewalk cafes! It was, I must say, a stroke of genius. All that atmosphere, and I didn't have to do a lick of work. Just in the nick of time, Grandma and Grandpa Freeman blessed us with a surprise visit at the skating rink. Christmas Eve was saved!

Back home, Scott and I shared the Nativity story by the light of the tree, held hands in a circle as we prayed with the children, and then later served egg nog with nutmeg on top. I had even bought a card table so we could play table games just like a real Norman Rockwell family. What do you think about that? Not too shabby for a couple of Christmas Eve Scroo—er, greenhorns, I'd say. Maybe there's hope.

Christmas morning, though, was a little shakier. There were a few hurt feelings and tense moments over who got what and who didn't and episodes of "Mom always loved you best!" But for the holiday impaired-in-recovery, it's not easy to be gleeful two days in a row.

With this dilemma in mind, Scott and I have been mulling over the subject of New Year's resolutions. After all, just two days ago we tossed out the old calendar and brought in the new with its fresh pages promising new starts. I must confess that my standard New Year's resolution is to not make any New Year's resolutions. It's always too depressing when I break them. This year, however, we've decided to attempt a resolution or two. What can it hurt?

First of all, we would like to try lowering our "special occasion" expectations. Second, we want to work at minimizing the level of stress in our lives. Last night as we were lying in bed Scott made a profound declaration that is already helping me feel more relaxed.

"Becky," he said, "I think we have both decided we want a good marriage. And a long one. We've got a lot tied up in this deal. For all these years you've been the one who reads the books and tries to figure out what to do to make our relationship better. I think I'd like to give it a shot. I'll even make it one of my New Year's resolutions. I think I'll just read a few books and see if I can figure this marriage stuff out for myself, and then I'll let you know what we need to do."

I loved it but had to laugh. "So does this mean I'm fired from being the Head Relationship Figurer Outer?"

"Yep."

In a strange way, I'm finding the new arrangement a big relief. Trying to understand how to make our complicated, intense relationship work smoothly has certainly left me exhausted—and more confused than ever. I was more than happy to give Scott a "go" at it.

Whatever transpires, this should be an interesting new year. Glancing again at the new calendar, I see we are facing another holiday test very soon. In twelve short days, it will be—the birthday of Dr. Martin Luther King Jr.

Just thinking about Dr. King and his timeless speech made me realize that I, too, have a dream—a dream that a husband and a wife will walk hand in hand into one holiday after another with peace and joy and love and harmony in our hearts.

Next New Year's Eve, perhaps Scott and I will be able to gaze happily into each other's eyes, share an intimate kiss at midnight, and look back on nothing but warm and happy memories of the Christmas vacation when we learned a full year's worth about living. If so, rather than singing the familiar chorus of Auld Lang Syne, our children just might hear us singing triumphantly, "We made it at last! We made it at last! Thank God Almighty, we made it at last!"

Love . . . . Always . . . hopes.

1 Corinthians 13:6–7

TWENTY-ONE

Tucking good stuff in *each other's* mailbox too

For some strange reason, Spring has decided to give the South a special preview this week. Though our calendars plainly state that it is early January, balmy breezes are winding their way from the open backdoor to my desk. Just last week, we had snow and ice. Today it is eighty degrees, and I'm wearing a ponytail and shorts! Last night, as Scott and I lay in bed, he opened a window and, believe it or not, a *mosquito* flew in. A mosquito in the middle of winter!

And this morning I had an interesting off-season visitor to my bedroom. Others might have screamed; I simply stared him down until he slunk away. I'll admit he wasn't all that threatening. Most green lizards are harmless, but at the very least, this one had guts, lying there basking in the heat of my electric rollers. This particular lizard was an anole, cousin to the chameleon. They have long been son Gabriel's favorite warm weather toy. Outside on a maple leaf, they are a brilliant shade of green. But once Gabriel gets them in his warm little hand, the gorgeous color fades to a nondescript, ugly brown.

As I took a "spring" stroll this January morning, I thought about how much we human beings are like the temperamental little anole. How easily we absorb the atmosphere around us into ourselves. Scott and I, both being cut of ultrasensitive cloth, are particularly vulnerable to outside input. Our emotions fluctuate like crazy Texas weather according to what we happen to be hearing, seeing, and learning all around us.

Because of that, I'm getting picky, picky, picky these days about what I allow to come in and around my head. For the most part, Americans have the privilege of choosing what we hear, read, and see. It is my desire to make the most of that freedom by actively seeking out Good Stuff. Interestingly, I've found that when I do happen upon something wonderful—an uplifting book, an intriguing verse of Scripture, a funny tape, an interesting article, a beautiful piece of music—I almost always end up sharing parts of it with Scott. And he does the same for me.

It occurred to me this morning, that this tradition of sharing the Good Stuff with each other has become a gentle way of looking out for one another—a mutual feeding of the other's soul. Speaking of food, when I've been served a luscious dessert, my automatic response is to offer my husband a bite. I want him to experience the same deliciousness I'm enjoying. And so it is with life.

Part of my reason for sharing Good Stuff with Scott is selfish, I must admit. It's my attempt to try to drown out, or at least balance out, all the negative junk the media slings his way. Whether we realize it or not, we are both subconsciously affected by the Bad Stuff Out There (hereafter referred to as BSOT).

For example, I hate it when we watch a television show or a video where the female lead turns out to be a lying sneak. For the next few days, Scott will look at me suspiciously as if he's wondering what evil is lurking up my so-called innocent sleeve. As for me, I may have a frightfully realistic dream that my husband is involved with another woman—as a result of seeing a movie with a similar plot. No matter how much Scott assures me of his faithfulness, there's a little part of me that is unreasonably *furious* with him for a couple of days. If exposed to enough BSOT, even human beings start turning an ugly, nondescript shade of brown.

On the other hand, inspirational movies or books or experiences can have a profound "greening-up" influence. Scott and I were deeply moved by the movie version of *Shadowlands*, the poignant love story of C. S. Lewis and Joy Davidman. Having been reminded of the brevity of life, we held each other closer in the night.

At the end of a long day, when the busyness of the house begins to quiet, one of the moments Scott and I look forward to the most is the exchanging of our mental mailboxes.

How was your day? Wait 'til you hear this! Guess what I learned how to do today? What do you think about . . .

I look forward to these times, much as I look forward to opening the morning mail. You never know what might be in the box. And, like mail, it is so much more fun when there's some Good Stuff in there. There's nothing more discouraging than endless deliveries of overdue bills and "friendly reminders" for dental checkups. We want interesting chatty news from each other. Funny anecdotes are always nice. Words of thanks and verbal "cards" of encouragement are also appreciated. And love notes are a perpetual favorite.

Herein lies the secret of keeping Married-for-Life Conversations a brilliant anole-green pleasure, rather than an ugly anole-brown bore. To have interesting marriages, we must show our selves interesting. As individuals, we can't stop growing, stretching, and learning.

Every day other "letters" crowd Scott's "mailbox." Lots of it, pardon my French, is a bunch of BSOT. Therefore, I want mine to stand out. I want to be the juicy, attention-getting one. I purposefully try to notice the Good Stuff Out There (GSOT)—uplifting items of interest—and when the time is right, I tuck some of it in my husband's box. And I look forward to the surprises he brings home to me too.

Sometimes, however, it can be pretty risky to arm a loved one with certain new and interesting bits of information, even if you are pretty sure it falls into the category of GSOT. I'll never forget the grenade I accidentally tucked in Scott's mailbox a few months back . . .

You are a letter . . . written not with ink
but with the Spirit . . . on tablets of human hearts.

2 Corinthians 3:3

T W E N T Y - T W O

Just please—I beg of you—don't bore me!

After having been so "greened-up" by the movie *Shadowlands*, I decided to follow up by reading the book. All the while I was reading about this unlikely pair of lovebirds, I found myself tucking away favorite quotes and passages in my Scott-Would-Get-a-Kick-Out-of-This-Too mental file. When I read that C. S. Lewis and his intellectual companions often held their deepest theological discussions over mugs of beer in local English pubs, I chuckled aloud. I kept trying to imagine professors at a nearby seminary popping 'round for an after-class chat over a brew at a local pub. And I knew Scott would appreciate this historical tidbit about the esteemed author of *Mere Christianity.* My husband's always questioning traditional, Americanized approaches to Christianity. Actually he loves to question untraditional, un-Americanized approaches to Christianity too. He just basically loves to question any and all approaches to everything.

Just as I surmised, Scott did enjoy the morsel of Lewis trivia. Unfortunately, the next time we went to church, our Sunday

School class took up a serious debate on whether Jesus turned the water into real or benign grape juice wine. Scott always makes me nervous when controversial subjects are under discussion, but I was even more nervous when I realized I had just handed him a potential bomb with the tidbit about Lewis. It was unlikely he would be able to keep himself from pulling the pin.

Needless to say, sitting next to Scott during the Pseudo Wine vs. the Real McCoy Wine Discussion was about as much fun as taking a little swim at a shark convention with a nasty cut. Just before I slapped my hand over his mouth, I vaguely remember hearing my husband say, "Well, if you ask me, what we all need right now is a good beer to help everybody calm down."

The next time I go to a Sunday School class with my husband, I want a sign to wear around my neck that says, "The opinions expressed by the man sitting next to me are not necessarily those of his wife. Actually, you can't be sure they are actually his own either. He just likes to keep things interesting."

Right now Scott is reading a book that compares marriage to the art of deep-sea fishing, and he is marking passages he wants me to read later. I'm reading James Herriot's latest book and getting a tremendous kick out of this country vet from Yorkshire. Every so often I have to stop to read a passage aloud for Scott's entertainment—using my best Cockney accent. We both listen to talk radio fairly often, so there's always the latest political hot topic to discuss. I never know whether Scott's going to come home sounding like Rush Limbaugh or a Bleeding Heart Liberal.

What am I trying to say? After all these years together, we continue to value what is in each other's noggin. And because the world is full of new things to learn and share, how could we ever get bored with one another? Hate one another, maybe. Disagree with one another? Oh, yeah. But become bored with each other? Unthinkable.

When I went back to college to complete my degree a few years ago, I can remember saying to Scott, "I'm all right with a professor who doesn't believe *anything* that I believe in—even if he challenges all my treasured values. At least he provokes my thinking. I'll even take a professor who is rude and obnoxious. But I can't *stand* a professor who stands up there and bores me to tears! I want to scream, 'Do SOMETHING! Say ANYTHING! But please, please, please don't *bore* me one more second or I will *explode* right here in this chair!' " Perhaps those same feelings apply to marriages.

Sometimes I tease Scott by telling him my life would have been so much easier if I had just married a boring couch potato. I've wondered what it would be like to live with a low maintenance guy who only needs a remote and a bag of potato chips to make him a happy camper. Scott is always looking for more—more excitement, new experiences, more intensity in our love. Quiet evenings at home are not his cup of tea. He likes to *go.*

Many evenings all I want is a hot bath, a quilt, and a good book. On the other hand, Scott is jumping up and down by the front door like a Chihuahua who's ready to go outside and play. More than once I've thought, *If only I had one of those little tranquilizer guns, I could just shoot him and put both of us out of our misery.*

But the real truth is, I'd much rather be dealing with a man who has an overly rapid heartbeat than one who is brain dead on the couch. At least I'm not bored.

For if I were, as you know, I might just explode in my chair.

An idle soul shall suffer hunger.

PROVERBS 19:15, KJV

T W E N T Y - T H R E E

The brain is a pretty swift aphrodisiac

This past summer, there was a fascinating article in *Life* magazine entitled "Brain Calisthenics." The article basically says that scientists have discovered that when people learn something new—even in their old age—their brain cells begin to branch wildly. This makes it easier for the synapses to fire and the entire brain to function better. It's like boosting the power in a computer.

The researchers also say the best brain exercise is to learn something unfamiliar. A mathematician might take up painting. An artsy, creative person might learn a computer skill. And the new area should require periods of focused attention.

So there's some news about how to keep our gray matter healthy. Now what does keeping our brain in good shape have to do with love? Interesting that you should ask. While I'm in this scientific mode, let's examine another theory that should help make the connection.

In his wonderful book *The Romance Factor*, Alan McGinnis points to another piece of intriguing research in his chapter entitled "Creating the Conditions for Ecstasy." He lists nine "triggers" scientists have found that will often precipitate feelings of joy, wonder, even ecstasy. By incorporating some of these triggers into our lives and our relationships, McGinnis believes we can live on a higher plane. Not only will we be more joyful as individuals, but also we will bring richness to our marriages. Some of the triggers include Music and Art, Natural Scenery, Play and Rhythmic Movement, Beauty, Sexual Love, Creative Work, and Religion. Another of those triggers is the Discovery of New Knowledge. Therein lies the answer to the question, "What does keeping our brains in good shape have to do with love?"

When our minds are growing—discovering new knowledge—we have more to bring to our relationships. It triggers new ideas to talk about, we become more interesting to be around, and we develop a more curious nature. We want to know our mate's opinion on a variety of issues, which makes them feel esteemed. We are not bored, so we are not boring. We also become more physically attracted to one another. An intriguing mind is a powerful aphrodisiac. The most successful mistresses have known this secret for ages. (So I've read.)

I realize as I write this that some people must be thinking, *Why is this classic "dumb brunette" writing about keeping intellectually fit?* Well, they have a point. But there is a difference between *absent*mindedness and *simple*mindedness. You see, my mind is not simple; it is just absent. Wait a minute, that doesn't sound quite right.

Anyway, I may be lacking in common sense, I may not remember to pull the cookies out of the oven on time, and I may find myself in circumstances to rival those of Lucille Ball's. None of that means I'm not smart. I was a member of the National Honor Society, even if I occasionally went to class with my dress on wrongside out.

There are several ways I keep the old gray matter moving while I'm doing intellectually stimulating things like moving the laundry from the washer to the dryer.

For one thing, I order lots of cassette tapes. I've attended at least twenty "seminars" while folding clothes or loading the dishwasher or taking a walk—seminars on marriage and family relationships, how to write and get published, self-esteem, in-depth Bible studies, public speaking, etc. You name the subject—somebody's taped a seminar and made a buck on it. Oh yes, I almost forgot! I also took a course on how to increase your memory. Can't remember the name of the course, but it was highly effective.

With so many books on cassette, I am also a much better driver. Now I can drive and "read" by listening to a cassette instead of driving and reading with the book on the steering wheel. The kids seem more relaxed.

There's also a wealth of learning available at local colleges. For mothers who dream of getting their degree someday, it may be possible to get a start on that dream sooner than they think. When my three oldest children were in school, I went back to college to finish my degree. Gabriel went to Mother's Day Out two days a week, so I used that time to go to class, and in three years I had a diploma. I loved college. I loved being around university kids. I loved the smell of new textbooks. I loved eating at the campus cafeteria and discussing new ideas and test scores and degree plans over coffee. I loved the whole enchilada.

The first time I went to college I was only seventeen and a newlywed. Scott and I had arranged to take all our classes together. We enjoyed the experience for the most part, but we were always irritated by one person in particular. It was the "old lady" student. You know the type. She was the woman in orange polyester who always sat on the front row and asked the professor a thousand annoying questions. She was always bucking for additional homework and destroying the curve for the rest of the class. However, when I went back to school at age thirty, I found *I* had turned into that "old lady." And I discovered another amazing fact—old ladies have a lot more fun with higher education. I also found out I looked pretty nifty in orange polyester.

Many churches have wonderful classes—with Bible studies that go beyond filling in one-word blanks. I've thoroughly enjoyed taking a couple of Precepts developed by Kay Arthur, and I understand that Bible Study Fellowship is also a wonderful source for those wanting to go into a deeper study of Scripture. Few things are as exciting as discovering a new truth or a significant correlation in Scripture—especially when you have to dig for it and know you'll get to share it with other women.

Meeting new people and getting together with old friends is another way to stretch the old brain and bring fresh news home to one's mate. When someone asks me what I miss most about my year of teaching, I always answer, "Lunch and recess." I loved the lunchtime workroom chats with my peers and I loved the relaxed playground chats with my little students. I think I learned more at lunch and recess than I did teaching in the classroom.

Now that I'm at home writing, I especially depend on my friends to keep me from feeling like a recluse and climbing the walls. Once a week, I meet with a few of my best friends for lunch—women my age whom I've known for several years. Then once a month, I meet with two local women writers whom I consider good friends. But they are also mentor-types. They're older, wiser, and much further along in their relationship with God than I am. And they both like chocolate. I believe, as a matter of fact, that a woman's spiritual maturity is in direct proportion to her affinity for chocolate. We are fast becoming an *incredibly* mature group.

A few months ago I began driving to Dallas to a once-a-month meeting of crazy, eclectic professional writers. Yes, you must be either crazy or eclectic or both to join. In this group are a couple of romance writers, a best-selling spy novelist, journalists and columnists for major newspapers, children's authors, screenwriters, computer nerd freelancers—and me. I am the token Naive Christian Humorist. With this crew there is always something exciting in the hopper—from big New York book contracts, to movies, to exciting publicity campaigns. I always feel like a kid with her mouth hanging open; I can't wait to get home and share the "buzz" with Scott.

Aristotle said, "To learn is a natural pleasure." I couldn't agree more. It's my goal for us to keep up with those brain calisthenics through the years. Unlike physical exercise, I actually find brain building kind of fun. I'm hoping by the time we are one hundred or so—even if our bodies have gone completely to pot—our inquiring old minds will still want to know. By then we'll need all the aphrodisiacs we can get.

To these four young men God gave knowledge and understanding of all kinds of literature and learning.

Daniel 1:17

T W E N T Y - F O U R

Love my kids, and I'm yours too

I once cross-stitched a sampler with the well-known saying, "The greatest gift a father can give his children is to love their mother." I might add that the reverse is also true: "The greatest gift a husband can give his wife is to love her children."

One evening not long ago, my husband stayed home with the children while I went to the grocery store. Shopping for a family of six when four of them are male takes a while, so it was late when I got home. When I walked back into the house, all was dark and unusually quiet. After setting down a bag of groceries, I tiptoed into the bedroom, lighted by the soft glow of the moon sifting through the window. Scott was lying there, his hands folded behind his head, staring at the ceiling. He seemed so pensive I immediately thought something was bothering him.

"Hey," I said softly and sat down on the bed beside him. "What's the matter?"

"Aw, I was just thinking about my daughter," he grinned sheepishly. "And how much I love her."

Evidently it had been a very good evening. "What happened with Rachel tonight?" I asked.

"Well," he sighed and searched for words to convey what he was feeling. "I had built a fire outside to burn some excess wood, and the telephone rang. It turned out to be a tough discussion with someone and I was upset. So I went outside to unwind by the fire, and, before long, our little girl came out of the house and snuggled by my side.

"'Dad,' she told me, 'you look like you could use a hug.'" He paused briefly and breathed a contented sigh.

"She's my little sweetheart, you know."

"I know," I smiled as I rubbed the back of my husband's neck. "And I hope she always will be."

The next evening Scott came home from work and found me asleep on the couch. He woke me by tickling my nose with a long-stemmed red rose. Before I could properly gush over it, Rachel strolled in from her room, beaming from ear to ear. Her strawberry-blonde curls boing-yoinging happily as she plopped down on the sofa beside me. In her small, slender hands she held a lavender basket of fresh daisies and pink carnations. Tucked into the arrangement was a card in Scott's handwriting.

"Thanks for the hug," it read.

Rachel's brown eyes twinkled, and she smiled triumphantly in my direction. "You just got *one* flower. Daddy gave *me* a whole basket!"

I'd say that little girl has got it made. I speak from experience. I am thirty-five years old and still a daddy's girl. But Lord help the first boy who asks Scott Freeman's daughter out on a date . . .

A couple of nights ago our family watched *Father of the Bride* on television. At the beginning, Rachel was sitting across the room from her dad. By the time it got to the scene where Steve Martin and his daughter play a final game of basketball together on the eve of the big wedding, Rachel was curled up under her daddy's arm. I don't know which of them wiped away the most tears. I do know I wouldn't take a million dollars for the memory of them snuggled together like that.

While Scott has his little daughter wrapped around his pinkie, he has Zach attached to Pointer, Zeke on the Ring Man, with Gabe holding onto Thumbkin. Last weekend, I watched Zeke help his father work on our house. Zeke voluntarily stays by his dad's side for hours most weekends, fetching and hauling and hammering and whatever it is that guys do to build a house together. Hardly a word passes between them—which is just the way they like it. Peace, quiet, good hard work with one's own hands—this is the stuff those two live for. Two peace lovers in a pod.

Later that same evening Rachel and I were eating a snack supper at the kitchen counter when Zach burst through the front door dressed in a camouflage suit, smelling of musty woods and crisp fall air. His dad followed close behind wearing a mischievous grin, which should have alerted us but didn't. Suddenly, the "boys" pulled a dead duck out their game bag and laid him with a flourish on the table in front of us. Rachel screamed and gagged appropriately, which I'm sure is what they were after. My snack didn't look so appealing after that, but it was worth it to watch Zach and Scott having so much fun together.

Then there's Gabriel. Age eight. All boy. The day after Thanksgiving, he asked his dad to bring the Christmas ornaments down from the attic. As fathers tend to do when asked to rummage through high, dark storage places on their day off, Scott brushed off Gabe's question, mumbling something about waiting a week or so. Not long after, I found Gabe quietly crying in a corner.

"What's the problem, Gabe?" I asked.

"Mom," he said earnestly, wiping away a tear, "I just want to *see* the ornaments. I'll put them away as soon as I look at them. I just want to see some *Christmas* today!"

What's a mother to do? I found Scott as quickly as I could and explained the gravity of the situation—that our son had to have a little Christmas right this very minute. Scott climbed up in the housetop, click, click, click. And down he came bearing gifts—a huge old popcorn can filled with Christmas treasures.

Gabe's lashes were still wet as he beamed up heartfelt gratitude to his father, the hero of the hour. Not to worry about me. It's my joy and privilege to stay behind the scenes in thankless anonymity.

Gabe's heart so overflowed with gratitude that he went to work right away making Scott's Christmas present. He tore a huge piece of cardboard off an old box and set about drawing a scene of his dad fishing. On the end of the crayon-drawn pole he pasted a real string and a real hook. Then came the inscription.

Dear Dad,

I Love you more than fish Love worms. I will never forget this christmost.

Love, Gabe

I loved seeing my child share open admiration for his daddy—even more than fish love worms.

The glory of children is their father.

PROVERBS 17:6, NKJV

T W E N T Y - F I V E

Insecurity and other irresistible qualities

I am a secure woman. I think. Oh, I don't know. Maybe not. But sometimes I wonder if other people think I think I am as secure as I think I think I am.

I guess I still have a few insecurities about the issue of my own security.

Today, for instance, I was feeling less than my best. I had a hard day. I was overwhelmed, discouraged, blue—and feeling very insecure. One thought kept coming to my mind: *I want my husband. I want to be held in his arms and hear him say everything is going to be just fine. I want to hear him say that I am not a failure.* Scott has become a physical and emotional refuge for me—a safe place where I can be engulfed by his loving arms and shielded from the world.

When he got home tonight, after holding me tight, he took my hand and led me outside. We walked about a mile, under the stars, and he let me talk until I felt better. Then he told me everything was going to be fine and that I was not even close to being a failure.

Is there any emotion more common than the feeling of insecurity? It is so easy—terribly easy—to be shaken from the treetops of self-assuredness. It's amusing really, how all our fine accomplishments can fade into nothingness with the slightest embarrassment or someone's casual hint that we might not be meeting the standard.

In 1868 Dostoevsky wrote, "If you happen to have a wart on your nose or forehead, you cannot help imagining that no one in the world has anything else to do but stare at your wart, laugh at it and condemn you for it, even though you have discovered America."[1] How easily do the mighty fall under the ax of imagined criticism.

One moment I believe I am all grown up, filled with the wisdom of the ages, with talent to spare. The next I am back in junior high, wondering if I'm ever going to be cool enough to fit in with the popular crowd.

Even the invincible Mark Twain appeared to be confused on the subject of self-doubt versus self-confidence. Once, with head and pen held high, he wrote, "A man cannot be comfortable without his own approval."[2] Of course that was in an essay written for the public. Nearly thirty years later, in the privacy of his notebook, he wrote, "We are offended and resent it when people do not respect us; and yet no man, deep down in the privacy of his heart, has any considerable respect for himself."[3] Maybe with the passing of years Mark Twain simply grew more comfortable—more secure, shall we say—with admitting his own insecurities.

Hey—wouldn't it be ironic if the sign of a truly secure person is his ability to admit his insecurity? Actually, there's a potential "immortal quote" in that question: "A man's security is in direct proportion to his ability to admit his insecurities"—a wise and profound statement by Becky Freeman. Perhaps it could even be cross-stitched.

In a good marriage, the partners are *always* sensitive to each other's insecurities. In *somebody's* good marriage anyway. Rather than poking fun at each other's foibles, they consistently reassure each other of their individual worth. We're trying to improve our average on this particular Good Marriage Test, and, actually, I think we are beginning to get fairly high marks.

I've had more than a few personal experiences over the past few years that have left me feeling somewhat insecure, including one or two booksignings.

I am crazy about bookstores, but I'm more than a little nervous about booksignings. If there is a nice group of friendly faces lined up at the table, it is hard to beat a booksigning for an afternoon delight. However, if nobody comes, it's about as much fun as being the last one picked for a baseball team in P.E. class.

You see, most of today's busy customers in large bookstores want to be left alone. Book browsing is a quiet, private affair and I, of all people, understand this. Who needs the pressure of a not-so-well-known author hawking her book in the middle of the store? But oh, the agony of being the mid- to unfamous author in the center of the store sitting behind a draped table, with a pen and a stack of one's books—and still being completely ignored. I've discovered people will walk twenty feet out of their way to avoid making eye contact with me in this situation. After a long, lonely stretch, I once thought about holding up a sign reading, "Will Autograph Books for Food."

Mother and I once spent three hours in a bookstore where no one bought our book except the owner of the store, who finally took pity on us. Eventually, however, a couple of friendly women walked though the front door and straight up to our table. It seemed obvious by their smiles and faces that they recognized who we were.

"Hey, Mother," I whispered, "here come some live ones." After exchanging the warmest of greetings and names of each other's grandchildren, the ladies politely asked if Mother and I could point them to the location of the reference materials.

Was I ever ready to be hugged when I got home. But I'm not the only partner in this marriage who suffers from occasional spells of insecurity. Scott also has his bad days . . .

It all began a couple of weeks ago when Gabriel came home from his Cub Scout meeting toting a little box containing a rectangular block of wood, two axles, and four plastic wheels. Little did I realize the momentous significance of that box. But as soon as Gabe showed the wooden block to his oldest brother, Zachary, I knew this was one of life's Big Deals.

As Zachary tenderly stroked the rectangle of wood, a faraway look came to his eyes.

"Gabe," he said wistfully, "you are in for the most special time of your life. I remember my first pinewood derby. Dad and I spent hours together sawing and sanding and painting my car. And I had the fastest car at the race. It was one of the best days of my life. Grandma even still has Daddy and Uncle Kent's first pinewood derbys from when they were little boys. It's the ultimate father/son experience." (Yes, my fifteen-year-old really talks this way at times. Even though he makes rude noises and standard fifteen-year-old obnoxious comments, he can also be surprisingly sentimental and eloquent.)

When Scott came home from work that evening, Gabe solemnly walked up to him. He was holding the piece of pine with both hands as if it were the Holy Grail and laid it in Scott's outstretched arms. I watched in fascination as Scott's eyes misted over. "Ah, Gabriel, my son. We have a race for which to prepare, do we not?"

For the next ten days, every evening was filled with pinewood strategy sessions. I could always tell Gabriel's whereabouts because I could hear the "shissh, shissh, shissh" of sandpaper smoothing the car to perfection. A shiny coat of black paint, a red pinstripe, and a fire motif completed the hot rod of pine. After drilling a few strategically placed holes and filling them with buckshot, the father/son drivers were ready.

On race day, Scott and Gabe dashed off early to get some graphite for the wheels. The rest of us—Zach, Zeke, Rachel, and I—joined them a little later.

When we walked into the rented fire station hall, I saw thirty little boys lining the walls, each holding a homemade hot rod in their sweaty little palms. Behind each Cub Scout was a father holding his son's shoulders with his sweaty big palms. The dads were all trying—with some difficulty—to look especially casual and nonchalant. But I knew, as did every other Cub's mother, that this was not only a testing ground for little boys' cars. The men were on trial for their fatherly racing know-how, intelligence, and influence. Successful Dadhood was on the line.

Gabe started out with supreme confidence. Even after his spiffy looking car lost the first race. Even after he lost the second race. But by the time he lost the fifth and sixth races, it was obvious that our little Cub was the owner of the Slowest Pine in the Woods. He was not only feeling insecure, he was also in the bathroom in tears. By that time, Mother Lioness was swallowing lumps in her throat. And Father Lion had joined his son in the bathroom. After comforting his Cub, Scott dried Gabe's tears and managed to get him back out on the race floor to help root for his teammates still left in the running.

Two hours later, we were back home and Gabe had recovered. As a matter of fact, a buddy came home with him and they were happily racing and comparing their cars in the back room. But my husband sat quietly on the kitchen bar stool, slumped over the counter, gazing blankly at the rain drizzling down the windowpane.

I handed him a warm cup of coffee and slid silently onto the stool next to him. He looked up at me with basset hound eyes, insecurity seeping from every pore.

"I lost the race," he said brokenly.

"Oh, Honey," I consoled, "you and Gabe had the *coolest* car."

"We lost the race. I let my son down."

"But your car *looked* the fastest."

"We lost *all* the races, Becky. Not just one or two of them. We lost *all* the races."

"I'm so sorry, Scott. What can I do to help?"

He stuck out his bottom lip. "Well," he sighed, "could I just have a hug?"

I was happy to oblige.

"Do you feel better now?" I asked as I gently pulled away.

"Well, yeah," Scott nodded, still looking pitiful. "But . . . um . . . I might need a kiss too."

"Oh," I smiled, kissing his forehead. "And is there anything else I can do for you?"

He was pouring it on thick now. Make-believe sniffs. Big exaggerated frown. But his hands massaging my back betrayed his sad performance. Father Lion was feeling his masculinity coming back again—and what was a lioness to do but respond to him in his hour of need.

When nobody comes to our party or we lose the Big Race, we need to be held—we need some refuge. From our experience, may I offer this helpful "freebie" tip? A tad of pitiful insecurity at just the right moment, and played in just the right way, could work to your advantage. Never forget that famous quote by that immortally insecure woman: "A man's security is directly proportionate to his ability to admit his insecurities."

What woman can resist a pitiful, playful, insecure, secure man with a touch of little boy-cub in him?

For You have been a strength . . . to the needy in his distress,
a refuge from the storm, a shade from the heat.

ISAIAH 25:4, NKJV

T W E N T Y - S I X

Look, I never promised you a thornless rose garden

(Or did I? I can't seem to remember . . .)

Am I losing my mind? Or does every mother of four seriously think she is getting Alzheimer's? This afternoon I received two phone calls that left me worried about myself again.

One was from Colyer, the competent publicist at Broadman, calling about an interview for the month of April. "This will be just before you leave for Phoenix, right?" Colyer asked.

"Right. Sure . . . Phoenix?" *Phoenix, Arizona?*

"Yes, I believe you've been booked for nearly a year to speak there."

"Oh, I see the problem," I explained. "I probably wrote the info down somewhere before I got this year's calendar. There were only a couple of things I needed to remember to put on the new calendar, so I'm sure I stuck them somewhere in the back of the old calendar and just threw it away when I tossed away the old year. Don't you think?"

Colyer was unruffled, as always. "Becky, I can always tell people that you really are the person you come across to be in your books," she said.

A few hours later, a lady named Ann called. All the time we were exchanging chitchat I was thinking to myself, *Ann . . . Ann. . . who is Ann?*

"I just thought I'd better call to make sure everything's on for next Thursday," Ann was saying.

"Yes," I stalled, "that's always a good idea. Can't be too careful." I cleared my throat and ventured, "Now, what is it that we have *'on' for next Thursday?"*

"You are speaking to our Garden Club."

"I am?"

"Yes, we've had you booked since last fall."

"Oh, well, *there's* the problem. You see, I threw away last year's calendar and I didn't have a "this year's" calendar last year, so the problem is that I didn't write it down on something I haven't thrown away yet. Does that make sense?"

She said she would understand as long as I showed up at the Garden Club next week with something witty and wonderful to say that would take up at least thirty minutes of the meeting.

Now my head is spinning because I'm overwhelmed. I'm already behind this week on my writing, and my deadline's looming large on the horizon. Why am I behind schedule? I had to go out to lunch with two sets of friends two days in a row because I believe in keeping relationships in good repair. And then, of course, this morning Zeke had a toothache, so I had to take him to the dentist, and on the way home we saw a used Blazer for sale. Since Zeke is totally embarrassed by the fact that I'm the only mother in the world who drives a Buick station wagon, we had to go for a quick test drive. I really liked that zippy little Blazer. Since it was eight years old I thought I could squeeze it into my budget. As soon as I got home I had to call the bankers and check interest rates on a used-car loan.

By the time I'd finished chatting with the bankers about the book I'm behind on writing, I'd lost so much actual writing time that I ended up negotiating one of those Desperate

Mother bargains with Zeke. If he would promise to clean the kitchen so I could catch up on the manuscript, I'd let him stay home from school the rest of the afternoon. He snapped up the offer. Just as I was about to settle down in front of the computer and get down to some serious business, the phone rang again. This time it was Zachary calling from the high school nurse's office.

"Mom, could you come get me? My stomach hurts and my head aches."

This time I turned into Selfish Corporate-Sounding Mother.

"Zachary, this is not a good time for me. Can we please reschedule this? Let's see, I have an opening for a kid with cold and flu symptoms next Tuesday. How would that work for you?"

"No, Mom! I'm doubled up with cramps."

"How doubled up? Are you just bending-over-slightly-and-whining doubled up or curled-up-in-a-ball-and-moaning doubled up?"

"Mom, I'm dying here! I'm lying in the nurse's office, writhing in agony on the floor!"

"Yes, I know, Son. But I'm really behind on my writing, and I've just been reminded of the fact that I have to go to Phoenix—you know, the one in Arizona—and now I've got to come up with a little talk for a Garden Club I also forgot about and—hey, guess what?—I'm in the middle of buying a car all by myself without even your daddy helping me. So, if there is any chance you are faking this sickness at all, I think it would be a very good idea for you to confess now."

"Mom, I'm going to call 1-800-CHILD-NEGLECT if you don't come get me right this minute!"

"Okay, but you'd better look really green around the gills when I get there," I said, dropping the phone in its cradle.

As long as I wasn't going to be winning any Mother of the Year awards anyway, I threw caution to the wind tonight and called in all favors from my husband with whom I've had a two-day "spat" a-brewing.

"Oh, dear, forgiving husband," I said sweetly over the phone, "It seems as though I've gotten myself in a wee bit of a bind today, and I thought I should just call you and let you know my head is about to burst from the stress. Is there any chance that you might come home early and take three healthy children and one slightly green teenager to the movies tonight?"

"OK," he agreed, "but you owe me one. Hey, wait a m-inute—I thought we were fighting."

"We are. But this just shows you what a desperate woman I am. Look, in a couple of days when we make up for all the things you did wrong, I'll be really, really nice about it. I'll never forget this favor—ever—if you will remind me. But you might want to write it down on my 'this-year's' calendar, just in case."

Bless him. My husband is, at this very minute, hauling our kids to see *Little Women*—a movie I'm sure all he-man types have been dying to see for some time now. Anyway, I'm thankful. He came, he took, I con-curred. And I now have an entire evening to ponder all the things I've forgotten.

Where *do* the remembering-impaired go for help? This can be a serious condition—with disastrous consequences. I confessed the enormity of my problem to a group of friends last week.

"Oh, come on, Becky," they said in cheerful unison, "it's not *that* bad."

They knew me well, but I could see I would have to produce some evidence.

"Look, you guys, I forgot my purse a couple of weeks ago on my way to an appearance on 'Good Morning Texas!' It was my first time to be on "TV" and I was frantic. I had to ask Scott to meet me on the road with my purse at 5:30 A.M."

"Well, that's pretty bad," they agreed, "but we've all done things like that. It's not as if you've ever forgotten a *child* or something!"

There followed a deafening silence. All eyes were upon me, waiting for me to join in the chorus of "Yeah . . . at least I've never done anything as horrible as *that!*" Finally, one brave soul asked, "Becky, you never really forgot one of your own *children?*"

"Well . . ." I stammered around for an excuse, "I hadn't had him very long! I'd just given birth to him a few days earlier, and I wasn't used to having four kids yet. I was having problems keeping count with the three I already owned. Anyway, we went to a frozen yogurt place and ordered cones. Zach, Zeke, and Rachel were sitting across from me, their sticky elbows upon the table, happily licking their treats. Out of the blue, three-year-old Rachel had a thought.

"'Hey, Mom, why can't we bring the baby in the store?'

"My eyes flew open, and I jumped from my seat in the yogurt shop to the parking lot in one incredible leap. Thank the Lord, Baby Gaby was safe—and sound asleep."

When the expressions of disbelief died down, I finished the sordid story.

"For months afterwards the kids kept reminding me, 'Remember you have *four* of us, Mom.'"

Now I know that many people, besides myself, have trouble remembering names. Sometimes I will be telling Scott about one of our *own children* and I'll say something like, "You wouldn't believe what—oh, shoot, what's the name of that kid? He's second to the oldest, and it rhymes with 'meek' . . . yes, thank you . . . you're right, it's Zeke. Well, you wouldn't believe what Zeke said the other day . . ."

Yesterday I suffered a most embarrassing moment. I was having lunch with two friends, Fran and Gracie. I've known these women for nearly two years now and meet with them monthly. Over a cup of coffee, Fran began relating a terrible personal tragedy of gigantic proportions. I was deeply moved and gazed into Fran's eyes with great compassion.

"Oh, *Gracie,*" I sighed. "I'm so sorry."

Gracie, sitting across from me, observed all this and gently said, "Becky, honey, I'm sure you *are* deeply sorry. But *I'm* Gracie—that's *Fran* you're talking to there."

At that point, all three of us laid our heads down on the table and laughed 'til we nearly cried. It just goes to show you that critically forgetful people are still capable of bringing joy to others—in their own way.

As I contemplate all the things I've forgotten, it is amazing I've ever been able to accomplish anything. Writing with Mother was always disconcerting because I kept forgetting where I put our latest chapters. Interviews have been another challenge. Early one morning last fall, the phone rang and I reached over to answer it. A deep voice on the other end was making an announcement: "And here, on the air with me today is one of the authors of *Worms in My Tea*—Becky Freeman! Well, Becky, how *are* you this morning?"

"Um . . . actually . . . I'm a little fuzzy . . . ," I managed as I worked to clear the morning frogs out of my throat. Yes, I'd forgotten the radio interview.

I've whispered quiet thanks time and again for the fact that my books have played up the fact that I am absentminded—it's considered a humorous device. That way, the mistakes and flub-ups I continue to make in the public eye are all a part of the character. It's a pretty good arrangement. What if I had written a how-to-be-together-like-me book?

Maybe my "forgetfulness issue" is simply destined to be a permanent thorn in my side. Right now, in some movie theater with four kids spilling popcorn all over him, Scott probably sees my little problems as a thorn in his side, too. But herein lies another lesson in marriage.

(Now all I have to do is remember what it is.)

Oh, yes—the lesson is that when we marry someone, our "thorny problems" also affect them. To me, a true "thorn" is a fault with which one seems to be permanently afflicted—no matter how many organizers one buys and promptly loses. But I must admit it does seem a shame that my innocent bystander spouse is often "stuck," if you will, with the fallout from my prickly thorns.

However, I've noticed something. It seems to me that most wise, old, happily married couples have resigned themselves to accepting a few of each other's sticky habits and personality traits. Either they've accepted the "thorns," or they've decided to downplay their seriousness in light of their loved one's other more rosy qualities.

I will probably always battle my "thorn of forgetfulness" to some extent, no matter how hard I work to compensate. And Scott will always battle a few of his thorny old faults too—though I can't seem to recall exactly what they are right now. See—there is a positive side to forgetfulness.

Oh, wait. I just remembered one of his faults. He crunches and slurps his cereal in a most irritating way. I've instructed him time and time again about correct cereal-eating etiquette, but—to no avail. I thought about not allowing him to eat a bowl of cereal again, but then I decided I would just have to deal with it. So when he gets out the box of cereal, I go take a bath and turn the water on "high" so I can't hear the "crunch, crunch, slurp—crunch, crunch, slurp."

My concluding advice? Stop and smell the roses whenever you can 'cause, honey, you're gonna need to remember how pretty they were and how good they smelled when you come across each other's thorns.

And when I forget my own advice, somebody please feel free to remind me.

"Can a woman forget her nursing child . . . ? Surely they may forget, yet I will not forget you. See, I have inscribed you on the palms of My hands."

ISAIAH 49:15–16, NKJV

TWENTY-SEVEN

I still "have it"

Can we talk? We've hung around together for several pages now. I think we can be honest with each other. I have a rather personal question: Does anyone else out there ever wonder whether or not you still "have it"? Not, of course, that you'd ever want to *use* it. But let's suppose something happened to your better half, and after a few years of grieving and loneliness, you absolutely had no choice but to go out there and reel in another mate—do you think you'd still have what it takes to get him on board?

In our heart of hearts, I think most married folk secretly ask themselves this question on occasion—especially when our own marriages seem lackluster. It often seems to surface when we reach our mid-thirties or early forties—the classic "mid-life" syndrome, I suppose. Well, I've reached my mid-thirties and, just for the record, it's nice to know—I mean I am absolutely *certain*—that I still "have it." I could still snatch another male in record time if I should find myself suddenly alone. The only problem is that my "catch of the day" would be over the age of seventy. With this select population of men, I am a hands-down winner.

In all fairness, I probably owe my ability to attract men-living-on-social-security-and-creamed-spinach to my mother. Her affinity for cafeterias has been well documented, but did I ever mention the fact that she had a "boyfriend" in every Luby's cafeteria? And she's been none too discreet about it either. I remember one conversation in particular between my parents.

"George," Mother began, trying not to look pleased, "it happened again. At the cafeteria. A nice, older gentlemen just couldn't keep his eyes off me. Then he followed me to the cash register and asked me if I was married."

"Ruthie, Ruthie, Ruthie. If I've told you once, I've told you a hundred times—quit batting your eyelashes at the senior citizens."

"I know George, I just can't help smiling at these men. They look so—lonesome. I think what they really like about me is my hair. Not many women wear their hair long and in a bun anymore. I probably remind them of their mothers. Yes, I think that's it. They like my bun."

Daddy slowly lowered his newspaper and raised his eyebrows. "Without a doubt," he agreed.

Even when they moved 1,500 miles away to Virginia, it only took my mom about two weeks to find a new, aged admirer at the local cafeteria. It was uncanny.

Now I'm the same age my mother was when she began giving old men heart palpitations as she floated by, and I'm discovering I am my mother's daughter for sure. For I, too, am now attracting elderly men at every turn. I don't think it is my hair, either—for though it is long, it isn't bunned.

I just know I have it with these old guys, but what exactly is this mysterious "it"? I'd like to think that it is my friendly smile or my rather "voluptuous" figure. (I've heard that many men from previous generations preferred their woman with a little more meat on their bones. Ah, the good old days.) Yet there is something about this that worries me. These graying men may think they are going to have to lower their standards of perfection if they—at their age—are going to catch the eye of a younger woman. So what if, when I walk by, they are actually thinking something like, "Now there goes a little chickadee even *I*, at age ninety-seven with no teeth, might have a chance with. I doubt she could do any better considering her mid-thirties condition and all."

I think I'll just not worry about it. When a woman gets to be my age and is trying to make peace with her own older, wider, more wrinkled "body model," she takes all compliments at face value. A compliment is a compliment, and I need all I can gather at this stage of the game.

Now I haven't frequented cafeterias quite as often as Mother, so for me this phenomena started with older fellows who worked behind counters. I'd be friendly to them as they counted out change, and before I knew it they were hooked. If I didn't come into the store for a week, they'd act crushed—as if I weren't showing enough interest in our relationship. Running in for milk and bread or a roll of duct tape became complicated.

Away from home, I ran into similar problems. On a late night trip home from Houston, Scott stopped at a burger place so I could run in, get a cup of coffee, and go to the restroom. I was wearing a peasant blouse and a Mexican-style skirt, but keep in mind that I had also been asleep in the car up until that point. This meant I had smeared my eyeliner, drooled off my lipstick, and my hair was packed into a large, flat pancake shape.

But as I walked in, I noticed immediately that there was an older gentleman working behind the counter. He looked to be in his mid-eighties. I ordered a cup of coffee, trying to cover my morning breath as I gave him my order. He asked me if I knew what an attractive woman I was. (I checked his eyes for signs of cataracts.) After an interesting parley, he finally handed me my coffee—with plenty of cream and sugar, if-you-know-what-I-mean.

As I turned to leave, the charmer asked me where I was going. I told him my family was waiting in the car. He gave me an exaggerated "don't leave me now" look before signing off with a wrinkled wink. I hated to snag his heart like that and then leave town, but when you've got it, you've got it. And in situations like this, what's a woman with a lot of "it" to do?

As exciting as my over-the-counter encounters have been, they've been nothing compared to the delightful conversations I've had with elderly men in bookstores. First of all, I should explain that my idea of paradise would be to be snowed in for a week in one of those huge bookstores that serve gourmet coffee and cheesecake. If I have a free afternoon in the big city, you can find me browsing through aisles with an armload of books and a silly grin on my face. And often, I end up running into elderly men who seem to be browsing for a younger woman with an armload of books and a silly grin on her face.

My favorite encounter was with an elegant, white-haired, bearded gentleman. He was slim, tall, and impeccably dressed—starched white shirt, plaid suspenders, red silk tie, and tweed dress slacks—like a distinguished old professor out of an English novel. As I was scanning the "relationship" section of the store, the elderly man approached with twinkling eyes and a charming smile. He was holding a piece of paper tightly in his hands. He looked from me to the paper to the shelves and back to me again before finally gathering the courage to clear his throat. As I glanced in his direction he made a slight bow and ventured, "Excuse me, madam, but do you think these books are listed by the title or by the author?"

I was pretty sure he knew the answer to the question, but I replied in my most sweetest and most helpful tone, "I believe they are listed by author."

"Oh . . . well that won't help me much . . . I only have the title here with me."

He held out a slip of paper for me to read. The book he was looking for was called something like *Say It Right the First Time.* I was curious. I hadn't imagined, at his age, that communication would be a problem. I was intrigued by his desire to improve himself. Then I remembered his dilemma.

"Sir, if you tell the lady at the front desk the name of the book, she can look up the author and location for you on her computer."

"Oh," he stammered, obviously not in any hurry to head toward the front desk, "You've been most helpful . . . most kind. Um . . . my name is Manning. May I ask yours?" As he extended his hand, I put mine out for a shake, which turned out to be more of a gentle squeeze. I thought for a moment he might bring my fingers to his lips for a kiss. Blinking myself back to the question at hand, I answered:

"I'm Becky." (I was careful not to give him my last name in case he fell hopelessly in love with me and might try to look me up later. I learned all about Stranger Safety when I taught first grade.)

"Well, Ms. Becky, tell me what book you are looking for so I may return the favor and help you." *(So he did know his way around the store—just as I thought!)*

"Well, actually, I'm doing some research for a book I'm writing on marriage."

"Oh, my! You mean to tell me you're an author! How lovely! And I must say, I've always been *fascinated* by the male/female relationship."

"Is that so?" I asked, flattered by his enthusiastic response.

"Oh, yes. I've taught anthropology and have studied the primates for years—I've especially enjoyed comparing their mating habits to those of Homo sapiens. You know, in the wild, female gorillas always seek out the strongest, most handsome male. Several females, one powerful male. Stimulus, response. Same thing with people, you know."

Hmmm. I wonder if this old fellow fancies himself Top Gorilla, I thought to myself.

"Well, yes," I answered, wondering all the while what in the world I was doing discussing the mating habits of gorillas with an elegant old chap in the middle of a bookstore. However, ending up in odd places is a pattern with me, so I plunged on.

"Manning, I have to take issue with you on one point. I believe there is something that makes human beings uniquely different from the animal world. For humans, between stimulus and response, I believe there is *choice*."

Manning smiled and said, "Interesting theory. You've obviously given this some thought. Tell me now, what advice would you give a babbling old man on how to grow up?"

"I think I'd tell him, 'Don't be in too much of a hurry.'"

"I like that. I've always said it is important to have a childlike, downright *indecent* curiosity about life. I find the world a fascinating place in which to live, full of fascinating people—like you, for instance."

I wisely avoided asking him what other "indecent things" he might be curious about and steered our discussion in the direction of home and family. He had lived in France, England, Wales, and Scotland. I should see the marvelous libraries of Europe someday, he said. I found out he was married—for twenty-four years, in fact. "That's a pretty long marriage," I commented, hoping to gather some encouraging advice for this book, perhaps. It was not to be. "Yes," he answered, "Unfortunately the first one lasted even longer than this one."

After a few more minutes of conversation, I glanced at my watch. Manning's face fell, and I felt sorry for hurting his feelings with my "I'm-in-a-hurry" gesture. But he spoke softly, allowing me a graceful exit.

"I see that you are thinking about taking your leave. But I must tell you, Ms. Becky, I'm truly sorry to have this conversation come to an end. It has been positively marvelous making your acquaintance." After shaking hands good-bye, I walked out the door, smiling to myself.

It surprised me to find my heart fluttering like a school girl—if only for a split second. Not only did I still have it, but this seventy-plus man *absolutely* still had it. Charm is charm at any age. Flattery works wonders, transcending generations. If I were his wife, I don't believe I'd let this debonair bookworm wander unaccompanied down aisles of large bookstores.

Scott has never begrudged me my gentlemen admirers. The way I see it, Scott is actually a very lucky man. He can rest assured that no matter how old he gets, or how senile he becomes, he will always be Top Gorilla as far as I'm concerned. How do I know? He's got charm, and he's got his following of cute little old lady admirers. If this mutual admiration of senior citizens holds steady, the older we become, the more attractive we will be to one another. We've got a lot to look forward to in our Golden Years, and I'm ever so glad we're headed that way together.

They shall still bear fruit in old age;
They shall be fresh and flourishing.

PSALM 92:14, NKJV

TWENTY-EIGHT

A little slapstick livens up dull days

Just when I think my life is growing dull and I'm running out of material, something seems to fall in my lap from out of nowhere.

It's a laid-back Sunday evening. Or at least it was. The family seemed content and all of them looked happily occupied. Some were sprawled on the living room couch watching a movie, one was soaking in the bathtub, another reading a book. So I thought I'd sneak off for a few minutes to work on this manuscript.

Suddenly, the body of a large man fell against the door, knocking it open as he collapsed at my feet. I recognized him as my husband. He had contracted into a fetal position, holding both legs against his chest. As I helped him to the couch, he winced, and through his clinched teeth I understood him to say, "You'll never believe what I did."

"Oh? What makes you think I wouldn't believe it, Baby?"

I cautiously untied his shoes and helped him out of his jeans. At this point he began to see the humor in the situation. He was laughing and moaning at the same time. I could see a large scratch across one thigh—and whatever it was that had given him the scratch had also torn through his jeans in the process. On the other leg, a large goose egg was already beginning to swell on his right kneecap. It hurt to look at it. I ran into the kitchen for ice and asked Zeke to help me move his dad into the living room, where I gave him a couple of pills for his pain.

Once we were able to assess my husband's wounds and had determined nothing was broken, I asked for details. "So would you like to talk about it now?"

"Well, it's really embarrassing," he said.

I thought of all the dangerous situations my husband had put himself into as he worked on our house every weekend—wiring high-voltage electrical circuits, lifting heavy beams, operating circular saws from lofty perches, and of course, hanging from the rafters by one hand with a caulk gun in the other. I thought to myself, *Nothing my husband did to injure himself would surprise me.*

I was wrong.

"Come on, Scott," I probed, "I promise I won't yell at you. What did you do this time? Were you trying to move that table saw without asking for help? Did you fall between the beams? Did the truck trailer collapse on you? What?"

He grinned sheepishly. "Remember that metal workbench I moved from the neighbor's house to our backyard today? Let's just say that while I was running around in the dark, I found it."

"Should I ask *why* you were running outside in the dark?"

"Maybe that wouldn't be such a good idea."

"Come on, I can't stand the suspense. Tell me."

"Well, you know how our septic system has been overloaded with all the rain we've been having? So, I thought I'd be frugal and go outside behind a tree in the dark and . . . well, you know. I'd just finished two large glasses of iced tea, so I guess I was in a hurry to get to the woods. That's when I ran into the workbench and turned a flip into the night air."

So collapsed was I with laughter that I laid my head on Scott's shoulder and wiped the tears away. He was in the same condition, though every time he laughed it also brought on a moan.

"So, Scott," I gasped, "what you are trying to tell me is that you nearly broke both legs trying to . . . "

"Yes. Are you satisfied now?"

"Yes. I am. I really am. Scott?"

"What?"

"Can I use this?"

"What do you mean?"

"Can I write about it?"

"Becky, you're like a vulture circling weakened prey. Every time anybody does anything stupid, there you are, like Lois Lane, with her pad and pencil. Am I nothing but *material* to you?" But even as he said it he was laughing, so I felt pretty sure I was close to getting the go-ahead.

"Oh, Scott, you know I love you with all my heart and I am so sorry you are in pain. But how could you question my motives? Didn't I just give you my very own pain medication a few minutes ago?"

"What pain medication? I thought you gave me some Tylenol."

"Well, we're out of Tylenol. So I gave you some of my Midol PMS multi-symptom relief pills."

"What??? You gave me *girl* pills!?"

"See how cranky you are? You needed those pills. You'll feel much better in a few minutes."

"What do those things do?"

"Well, they keep you from fussing at those who love you."

"Is that so? And how?"

"They make you go to sleep and render you incapable of communication."

"Hmmm . . . Well, I *am* feeling kind of drowsy." His eyelids began to droop.

I waited a few more minutes before I spoke again.

"So it's okay with you, Honey, after you drift off to sleep and everything, if I go back out to my office and write about this?"

"Um . . . what? . . . I 'm so tired . . . whatev . . . "

"I'll take that as a 'yes,'" I said, and dashed for the computer.

As deadlines approach I find myself sounding more and more like an ambulance chaser, but I just can't help myself. As long as bad things happen, we might as well make the best of them and put it to good use. Right? Grist for the mill and all?

It's now the morning after the "accident." I rolled over in bed about 6:30 A.M. and woke my husband from his peaceful slumber by seductively wrapping my leg around his swollen knee. Honestly—I forgot! Once he stopped shrieking, he managed to get dressed for work. As he hobbled around in his pitiful condition, I asked him, "So, Scott, what are you going to tell the gals at work this morning about how you got your limp?"

"I'll say it was a skiing accident. Or maybe I got sideswiped by a truck. Which story do you think sounds more manly? "

"Well, don't worry," I answered, batting my eyelashes, "your little secret is safe with me."

"Suuure it is. I'll proofread the chapter tonight."

I love a man with a limp and a great sense of humor. One who doesn't take himself too seriously. One who is generous with potential humorous material. And who thinks I am witty too. As they say, "If you don't have a good sense of humor, get one."

I couldn't agree more. We could never have survived without the gifts laughter brings to our relationship. It is a diffuser, a stress-reliever, and a unifier.

Not long ago, Scott and I were lying in bed watching a scene from a romantic comedy. We both got so tickled we had to hang on to each other to keep from falling off the bed. We hadn't laughed that hard in months—it was one of those front-teeth-sticking-out, tear-wiping, side-aching sort of laughing spells. It felt especially good to be sharing it together.

Elizabeth Cody Newenhuyse, one of my all-time favorite writers, interviewed several couples for her book *Strong Marriages, Secret Questions.* She concluded, "The healthiest couples I interviewed were those who punctuated their remarks with wisecracks, understood each other's humor and frequently dissolved into laughter. Because life is funny . . . . It is also a powerful, and underrated, bonding agent."[1]

Life *is* funny. And unbelievably, it is getting even funnier at my poor husband's expense. It is now the *day after* "The Day after the Accident." A few hours ago, as I was putting my makeup on in the bathroom, the body of a large man fell against the bathroom door, knocking it open as he fell to the floor. Guess who? Same song, second verse. He was once again holding his knee and curled up in the fetal position.

"Oh, Scott," I said as I helped him sit up. "What have you done now?"

"Well, it's embarrassing," he moaned, gingerly examining his wound.

"It's broad daylight, please tell me you weren't looking for a tree . . . "

"No, no, no. It wasn't that bad. This time, I just whacked my leg with a two-by-four."

"Hold on a second, don't say another word. You hop in the tub and soak your knee while I run get a pad and pencil."

I was back in a flash.

"OK, Scott. Now tell me again what happened, and don't leave out any details."

"Well, there's not much to tell, really. I was trying to get the porch post aligned, so I picked up a two-by-four and gave the post a few hard whacks. Only on one of the back swings I whacked my sore leg."

My husband seems to be stuck in a painful slapstick comedy routine. And here he was, *literally*, slapping himself with a stick.

I am truly sorry he's in pain, but you have to admit, he's been entertaining.

Somedays it's really a lot of fun to be married.

I delight in weaknesses, in insults, in persecutions, in difficulties.

2 Corinthians 12:10

TWENTY-NINE

Love me tender and get away with just about anything

Men should know that women sometimes get together and play a game called "Let's Compare Husbands." It's a lot like poker. And, as with face cards, not all hubbys' personality traits have equal value. According to the rule book, having the correct combinations is also important. I've played a few rounds myself and have had some pretty stiff competition, but usually I'm assured of having at least one ace in the hole. This is the way it goes.

"All right, girls," Player Number One says, "I'm holding a man who picks up his own socks and knows how to whip up a box of macaroni and cheese by himself."

"Wow," replies Player Number Two. "That's going to be a hard pair to beat. But I'll raise you. My husband can unstop a backed-up commode and doesn't mind changing the cat box."

"Oh, you're kidding!" says Three. "You've got a man with a strong stomach? All I've got is a regular paycheck coming in, a great father to the kids, and no snoring at night."

"Well, ladies," I say as I lay down my cards with a flourish. "Read 'em and weep. I've got a husband who's stubborn, knows how to say just the wrong thing at just the wrong time, and has the patience of a gnat. But when he's good, he's very, very good. He is tender. He is playful. And girls, I'm sorry to have to tell you this, but—he's also Romantic with a capital R."

"Oh, pooh!" the rest agree. "Becky wins again. It's not fair when she's always holding the King of Hearts."

I may be *slightly* overstating the case, but I haven't yet met a woman who wouldn't trade neatness and steadiness for a man who enjoys candlelight dinners, interesting conversations, and romantic waltzes.

I know there are many men out there who think Romantic equals Softness which, in turn, equals Big Sissy. Most of these men, unfortunately, are dateless, divorced, or sleeping on the couch. Take it from me, the surest way to a woman's heart is the most direct route—go straight for the heart.

Scott's natural ability to bring out the heart—the real depth—in people is one of the most attractive and, I think, romantic of his qualities. As hard as it is for us to control our tempers when things get out of hand, there is no way we can break off this relationship. There are too many topics we still haven't discussed into the ground.

Not long ago, our oldest son Zachary looked at me very seriously and said, "Mom, Dad is deeper than anybody I know. He's, like, deeper than the deepest well."

And Zeke, our second born, is so much like Scott it is almost spooky. Both of them have rather soft voices and a slightly hesitant way of speaking, but don't let that fool you. Not long ago, Zeke and I were talking in the kitchen. He was perched on a bar stool and I was actually *cooking*.

"Mom," he said in his newly husky voice, "I have all these deep, meaningful thoughts. But it is hard for me to say them. I don't have a way with words like you and Zachary. But I have all these really important thoughts." He paused for a second and then added softly, "Dad understands."

Both our boys have told me they love the way their father treats them—like real people with profound minds and interesting ideas, not like dumb little kids. A man who can make *teenage boys* feel significant and intelligent and respected as individuals has a gift.

Then there is music. A woman can tell a world about a man simply by finding out what sort of music he likes and how he responds to it. When it comes to music, Scott's affinity for soulful romance is off the charts. Listen to "When a Man Loves a Woman" and you've got my husband pegged. He's the type of man who will turn up a sexy song on the radio in his truck (parked in our driveway) and come running into the house to pull me outside so we can dance together under the stars. Especially if there is a full moon. The same is true for me. I've pulled Scott out from under a car where he was working just to two-step to a love song in broad daylight—even while he was covered with grease.

Little hard to hold on to him, but we manage.

When I think of romance and tenderness in our relationship, I also think of the countless little things that add to our love. The way we fit together when we lie in each others' arms at night. We call it "spooning." Then there is the way we sometimes talk to each other like little kids just because it's fun. When Scott completes a special project on the house, he might come take my hand and in a boyish voice urge, "Come see my big roof!" After being out on the lake, he might come up to the back porch and holler, "Hey, Miss Peeky! Come see my big fish!"

There's something else I find romantic about my man. I know, down deep, my husband believes in me, and he would fight to the death to defend my honor. He's been tested a time or two, as a matter of fact, and no woman could ask for a more gallant hero. He is, and has always been, my best fan. When I sang for him the first time, he loved it.

"It's a gift from God, Becky," he coached. "Let 'er rip!" Ditto for my early attempts at writing and speaking.

And I must ask, how many men would allow their wives to write and speak about their personal, private lives—letting her poke fun at their crazy relationship for all the world to see? A secure man. A good sport. A man who trusts me to write with openness and humor, without guile.

As a matter of fact, he graciously reads my work while allowing me to stare at him, taking note of every twitch, every minuscule response. By some miracle, he is able to completely tune out the fact that my face is five inches away from his. He just pencils his critique as if I am invisible. Then he always tells me the truth—where the manuscript made him want to laugh, where it touched him, where he had no idea what on earth I was trying to say. One of his most common markings is R. T.—for rabbit trail. He thinks I tend to wander off the beaten path too often and forget where I'm headed. Once the writing project is a wrap, I can always count on one thing: He will be prouder of me than any other human being on the face of the earth.

I like this man. Very much.

I like the perpetual conversation we have going. I like the little nuances of familiarity—baby talk, pet names, pet phrases. The mutual fan club. The meals we've shared—from greasy cafes to candlelit romantic restaurants. And perhaps, most of all, I've enjoyed the slow dances to beautiful music under the stars.

One of the most tender and touching stories of real-life married romance I've read is Madeleine L'Engle's book *Two-Part Invention: The Story of a Marriage.*

It is good, I think, for young couples to read and hear the stories of other long and romantic marriages. It puts a larger perspective on minor irritants we struggle with every day.

Ms. L'Engle is the famed Newberry Award winning author of *A Wrinkle in Time.* She was married to Hugh Franklin, whom some of you may remember as the handsome and distinguished actor who played Dr. Charles Tyler on the television show "All

My Children" for years. After forty years of a loving, intimate marriage, Hugh developed a terminal form of cancer. A lump still forms in my throat when I read Madeleine's account of holding her dying husband to her breast in his hospital bed as he took his last breath. She was unable for several moments to release her embrace. Then she turned to the doctor and spoke at last.

"It is hard to let go beloved flesh," she said.

Madeleine closes her autobiography with a beautiful line from a poem by Conrad Aiken, a poem Hugh had read to her some forty years earlier on the night he proposed marriage:

Music I heard with you was more than music, and bread I broke with you was more than bread.[1]

I cannot read those words without thinking of Scott, and I cannot think long on them without tears coming to my eyes. For one day I, too, may have to "let go beloved flesh." And when I do, it will be my husband's tender, romantic presence that I will surely miss the most. The presence that can make even everyday "bread and music" extraordinary.

"My beloved is . . . outstanding among ten thousand. His mouth is full of sweetness. And he is wholly desirable. This is my beloved and this, my friend.

SONG OF SOLOMON 5:10, 16, NASB

THIRTY

I know you love me, but do you *like* me?

I remember having a conversation with my mother when I was in my early teens. We were discussing one of Mother's friends—let's call her Mona—and the trouble she was having with her daughter—let's call her Jessie—who happened to be growing up into something of a snit, making life miserable for everyone around her.

"I know Mona loves Jessie," Mother sighed, "but sadly, I don't think she's ever really *liked* her very much."

It was the first time it occurred to me that parents, though obligated to love their children, might actually have a child whom they struggle to like. The thought made me uneasy.

"Well, Mother, " I questioned tentatively, "you like me, don't you?"

She laughed and gave me a hug. "I am absolutely crazy about you! You're one of the most fun things in my life, as a matter of fact. I get a kick out of you, Kid."

Whew, was I relieved. The conversation demonstrates, however, the importance of knowing we're not only loved but we're *liked for who we are.* And we human beings never seem to outgrow the need for such affirmation.

Now and again over the years, I've found myself not only asking that question of my mom and other people, but also of God. In truth, I think everyone comes to this point in life, probably many times. Sure, God loves me. The Bible makes that plain. But, does He like me? I mean, does He like *me?* And the answer found to that most basic of human questions colors every other relationship, especially the closest ones. Take the relationship with mates, for example.

If we believe God is just waiting to catch us in a mistake, we are more likely to judge our mates when they blow it. If we think God simply tolerates us, we may resign ourselves to merely "putting up with" our spouses. But if we could only *believe*, really believe, that God actually is delighted with us, that we are His adopted sons and daughters who bring Him joy even in the midst of our imperfections—that He *likes* us—wow! We could be free to really live. We could accept others and see through their faults and love them anyway.

I've been mulling over the whole biblical panorama lately and have asked myself, "Taking the whole lump of Scripture together, what is God's main, number one, heart's desire in it all?" I've come to some serious conclusions. Seriously. I have deep spiritual thoughts, you know, and a longing to understand the big picture. So, can I share with you what I'm "putting back in my box" these days? It has to do with the importance of believing we are liked by God and how that belief affects marriage and other relationships. First of all, I've come to believe that God's Plan A—what He wanted from the beginning—was simple, and somewhat surprising.

In the beginning of it all, God created the heavens and the earth, but His heart—ah, His *heart*—He poured into a plot of ground called Eden. He wasn't coerced into the idea; this was something He *wanted* to do. Then having done such a fine job with creation, He created a man and a woman to walk and talk with Him, companions He could love and *enjoy* in the cool of the day in this setting of astounding beauty. Adam and Eve, in turn, loved and enjoyed Him right back. God not only saw that it was good; He saw it was *very good.* In other words, He not only loved His children; He liked them—had fun with them, if you will. Plan A was, to borrow a popular phrase, the way things ought to be.

All through the Bible, from Genesis through Revelation, it is my belief that God's highest and best is still Plan A. All that happens in between is to get us back to the essence of the original plan, the plan that involved being not only a part of God's creation but His intimate friends. I heard Phillip Yancey, in a recent talk to our writers group, refer to this as "God's passionate pursuit of man." God Almighty, King of the universe, *wants* to be our friend. He not only loves the world; He *likes* having a relationship with us mortals, for some reason. (I still have a hard time comprehending that part, but what a great, wild thought!)

I will admit that *love* is the foundation for relationships, through good times and bad, but *like* is the stuff of joy and fun—and I really want both! As an example, I trust my husband will always love me, and that's great. However, lots of people have relatives they love but don't necessarily like. A friend of mine told me the other day, "Listen, Beck I love my in-laws, but to tell you the truth, it wouldn't hurt my feelings if I never saw them again." Who wants to be loved like that—only long distance?

If I'm honest with myself, what really gives me goose bumps is to feel I am liked by my husband, that he enjoys my company, that I double his pleasure when I am around. Who can resist a person who makes you feel liked? One of the highs of being married, actually, is falling in *like.* One of the highs of being a Christian, actually, is falling in like with God. We have to believe first, however, He wants to be our Friend and enjoys our company.

That's why Jesus came. He is our hope for getting back to Plan A. Interestingly, Jesus amplified the Father's desire for friendship with us. "Greater love has no one than this, that he lay down his life for his friends . . ." I no longer call you servants, ... Instead, I have called you friends" (John 15:13, 15). Soon after He spoke those words, He lived them. He walked up a long dusty road, with a heavy cross full of splinters upon His bleeding back, and gave His life for me, His friend.

Then early one Sabbath, in the cool of the day, Christ appeared to Mary, whose poor heart was breaking in two. Mary didn't recognize Him at first—at least not until He said one word that made her soul dance again. He simply spoke her name.

"Mary."

At the sound of her name coming from Her master's lips, she knew she had found her Friend again. Jesus continued to offer more tangible proofs that He *wanted* to walk, talk, and sup with those whose feet are sculpted of clay. The first thing He told Mary to do was to tell His "brothers" the good news of His return, not His backstabbing, cowardly, so-called buddies who betrayed him in less time than it takes a rooster to crow. He called the disciples His *brothers*—first "servants," then "friends," and then "brothers!" The Son joined the Father in the passionate pursuit of intimacy with man.

The next thing we know, Jesus was on a beach, cooking up a surprise breakfast for His old fishing buddies. As He called out the familiar, "Why don't you cast your nets on the other side?" the scene grew comical, fairly bursting with joy. Peter , hearing the voice of His Savior and Friend, could hardly jump out of the boat fast enough, swimming madly toward shore and, I'm sure, toward a bear hug to end all bear hugs. Later Jesus found a couple of guys heading to Emmaus and casually joined them in their walk, chatting about Scriptures, and going home with them for supper. Note how *human*, how *friendly* were His first encounters back on earth.

In all this, did He not make it all too clear that He doesn't want to love us from *afar?* He went out of His way to hang around a while just to let His friends know that no matter how they had blown it, He still liked them, enjoyed their company, and accepted them "up close and personal." If any questions remained about God's deep desire to pursue a friendship/love with us, Jesus removed all doubt in the garden of Gethsemene, and finally, in His resurrection.

In his tender and honest book, *Shame and Grace,* Lewis B. Smedes writes, "Grace is seen . . . full face in the story of Jesus. As I read the gospels, I am entranced by the simple and spontaneous way He accepted people heavy laden by their sense of being unacceptable."[1]

I've begun to notice that whenever I'm having the hardest time accepting my husband and kids—when I judge every move they make and become a demanding perfectionist—it's because *I* am drifting away from the simple truth that God accepts me as I am. Subtly, I'd started thinking again of Him as a menacing Being, waiting in the wings to catch me when I mess up. Only when I am filled with the assurance that He not only loves and forgives me but likes me as well—warts and all—do I find myself able to relax and enjoy my fallible self and family.

Malcolm Smith uses a wonderful analogy in his teaching series "Relationships that Last." In paraphrase, he says; "We all have a sucking, gnawing need to be loved and approved of by someone. The problem is, we're all going around like ticks trying to suck blood out of each other, but it can't be done because there's no dog! Human beings will never find their complete sense of love or identity in another human being. We need something other than ourselves—drawing on the love of God until we are immersed in the assurance that we are loved, we are loved, we are loved."

I would add only one postscript: Also we are liked, we are liked, we are *liked*. As hard as it is to believe, by the Creator of the universe. The trickle-down effect of accepting that fact is amazing.

Because people who are filled up—who believe they are loved *and* liked by God—are not only less threatening, they make much better friends and marriage partners than hungry ol' nervous ticks.

The LORD your God is with you, . . . He will take great delight in you, he will quiet you with his love, he will rejoice over you with singing.

ZEPHANIAH 3:17

T H I R T Y - O N E

For all good gifts around us

Remember "The Cosby Show" episode where Clair, mother of five, finally acquired a room to call her own? She spent the entire day alone in her newly remodeled room, stretching out on the fresh carpet, dancing with abandonment to music coming from her boom box, stopping only once—to order "room service" from her husband. Downstairs the children were dumbfounded. What in the world could Mom be doing up there all by herself? Wasn't she getting bored or lonely? My bet is that every mother smiled when she heard those questions.

What mother of multiple children hasn't dreamed of a room of her own behind a locked door? Something besides the bathroom. And during the preschool years even a chance at privacy in the bathroom is pretty iffy. I have been known to lock myself in the car on a Sunday afternoon, leaving the kids to their daddy, in order to read the newspaper.

But I have come to the end of that. It is over. Finished. Today is a Red Letter Day for me. At this very moment, I am working at a desk in my very own, brand new office. I have already rolled around on the new carpet. And it is as wonderful as I've always dreamed it would be.

So today I want to pause and thank the man who made all this possible: A Craftsman Extraordinaire—my talented husband. He built my beautiful room all by himself. From the fresh white paint, to the natural wood-framed picture window, to the ponderosa pine wainscoting, to the deep green marbled wallpaper with its rosy border, to the plush champagne-colored carpet, to the bright fluorescent lighting above my head. Every nail, every brush stroke, every jot and every tittle was done by my husband.

Actually, this is more than just a Red Letter Day for me. It has been a Red Letter Week. Remember the supercool Blazer that Zeke and I took a spin in? Believe it or not, I found an even cooler, "superer" sport utility truck parked in my driveway this week. A red rose was stuck in the steering wheel.

After Scott peeled me off his neck, he said he thought I'd probably gotten all the humiliating material I could squeeze out of the old panel station wagon, and now he wanted me to ride around town with my head held high when I plow down mailboxes and run into ditches.

I spent the entire next day tearing around country roads, stopping only long enough to phone Scott to ask if he had any long errands he'd like me to run. I told him I basically planned to *live* in my supercool sport utility vehicle for the rest of my life. It is *such* a relief to finally be cool.

And that's not even all the new stuff I got this week. I know it sounds like we must have just hit the jackpot, but, honestly, everything just seemed to come together at one time. It's been like Christmas in February for me.

Anyway, after nearly nineteen years of marriage, I received my first piece of truck-delivered furniture. Last November, I walked into a real furniture store and ordered a couch outright. I even picked out the fabric—a homey, rich, red plaid. But it felt so weird—like I was my mother, or a normal, settled grown-up or something.

All of our furniture has been either Early Marriage (out of some relative's garage) or Wal-mart pressboard and laminate specials—until my couch showed up at the door last week, that is. It's a name brand, too. La-Z-Boy. I love the sound of that. I like telling my friends, "Oh, that piece? Yes, it's new. A La-Z-Boy, don't you know?"

The seats on both ends of my couch actually *recline!* And the cushion in the middle flops down, turning itself into a handy snack table, though I've threatened to flatten any member of my family who dares to eat an actual snack there. There is also a nifty secret drawer where the family can store the remote control, magazines, books, and, more than likely, forbidden snacks they'll be trying to hide when I walk unexpectedly into the room.

I owe special thanks to my husband who could have easily whined about my spending money on a couch when it probably should have gone toward boards and sheetrock and tar paper or some other ugly but expensive things that we really need. You see, the entire family is very much looking forward to the day when we can tear down the walls of our cabin within a house and the six of us gerbils can all expand.

This week has been a remarkable week in the life of the Freemans. After so many years of barely making ends meet, we have realized that for the first time in our marriage we can actually breathe when we balance the income against the outgo. All that we have done without and worked so hard to build is beginning to take shape. We are becoming The Mama and The Papa and looking forward to the days when we will be The Grandma and The Grandpa. When we stand in our yard and gaze up at the house we are building together, and see the lake beyond, and realize the memories we already have of this place—our home—we don't even bother to wipe the tears from our eyes. And how do you thank God for genuine miracles?

And today, on this Red Letter Day of my life, the main thought that keeps running through my mind is, *What if we had quit too soon? Oh God, what if I had missed this?*

Every good and perfect gift is from above, coming down from the Father.

JAMES 1:17

THIRTY-TWO

Real-life vows for Bubba

Well, the latest news around here is that Bubba is fixin' to get hitched. And he's young, so Melissa, his mothering boss, is concerned.

First, I should introduce Melissa. She is a new friend—a gift from God to me in these boonies. She and her husband, Mike, have just moved into our neck of the woods and are operating this cute, country "village market" down the road. Melissa and I laughed the other day at how quickly we've become "kindred spirits and bosom friends." Melissa loves to read, talk about books and relationships, and laugh. She hates housecleaning, loves gourmet coffee and frozen yogurt, and worries about her weight. Not only that, but she and Mike have two charming, funny kids—Joshua and Sarah—who are terrific playmates for my kids. (That's JOSHUA GANTT and SARAH GANTT—who threw mortal fits to have their names in this book. Will that work, guys?) Anyway, Melissa read about me in my first book before we ever met, and she told me she knew right away we would relate. She was right.

But back to Bubba. Melissa is not unsympathetic to Bubba and his fiancée's desires. She and Mike, like Scott and I, met at church as preteens and married as teenagers. But she'd like to give Bubba a more realistic picture of what day-to-day marriage is like when you marry young.

Bubba is eighteen, as cute as cowboys come, and head-over-boots in love. He and his intended plan to be married right after her high-school graduation. Then they would like to go straight from the chapel to Happily Ever After. But Scott and I, and Melissa and Mike—all partakers of early marriage—know all too well that "happily ever after" only happens in fairy tales. "Happily here and there," maybe. Or "More happily than not," perhaps. But nobody, except Cinderella and Sleeping Beauty, gets Happily Ever After every day. So as a favor, Melissa asked me to add a chapter to this book so she can give it to Bubba before he ties the knot. She wanted me to write some *real* wedding vows. In other words, what's the real scoop behind the "I do's"?

So, Bubba, here's my best shot. For convenience's sake, I will use Scott and me as the sample bride and groom in this demonstration.

I, Scott, take thee, Becky, to be my lawfully wedded wife. . .

To have—That is, when you don't have a headache or aren't too tired from chasing kids all day or staying up all night with a baby. Since quantity and quality ebb and flow, I'll try to go with the flow and not whine with the ebb. And I'll try to remember that sometimes the sexiest thing a man can do for a woman is talk to her and listen to what she is trying to say.

And to hold—Even when you come toward me crying like a Water Wiggle gone mad and everything in me screams, "Run fast—in the opposite direction!" Because no matter what is wrong, I know, most of the time, that what you really want and need is to be held.

Being faithful only unto you—This means I will never, ever see or touch any other woman's naked body up close and personal. (Not ever? Whew, this is a toughie.) You will be it for me. The end of the line. But that's OK, because one real woman is all that I'll ever need. And I'll remember that to light your fire I've got to strike the match early in the day with tender touches and romantic talk.

In sickness—I'll do my best to be helpful and sympathetic, even when you have the kind of sickness involving vomiting and other disgusting unmentionables. I'll bring you a cool rag and tell you, "I'm sorry you feel so bad," in a sympathizing tone of voice. Until I get the hang of it, I'll call your mom and ask what I should do with you.

And in health—It may be somewhat of a challenge to stay healthy when you are first learning to cook—and everything is either burnt to a crisp or comes attached to a stick. But I can always run out for a salad. So I'll pretend I love burnt corn dogs and popsicle dinners because I care about your feelings more than food.

For richer—Realistically, we are going to be looking at a ten-to-twenty-year wait on this one—especially if we are going to put each other through college. But it will probably be even more years if at least one of us doesn't get a degree. In the meantime, we can dream together, can't we?

For poorer—This may mean sharing-a-small-cheeseburger-with-no-soft-drink-at-McDonald's poor. It could very well mean Ramen-noodle-soup-for-three-days-in-a-row poor. Perhaps even Salvation-Army-Clothing-Store poor. And we can't run up credit cards or go home crying to Momma and Daddy for more money every time the going gets tough. Together, we'll find a way to make it. But to be honest, we can probably expect to fight a lot about money on the way—especially when things are tight.

In good times—We'll have a lot of these if we can just remember how to play and have fun together after we are "responsible married adults." We'll need to get away for mini-vacations when the stress builds up—even if it is just going for a walk under the stars. And these good times will be so sweet we will forget about the rest of the world and its problems, at least for a while. I'll do my part in keeping it good by looking for the best in you and downplaying your faults. And I'll keep growing and stretching and learning myself because I want to help you do the same.

And in bad—Even when I wake up next to you one morning and you have no make-up on and your thighs look as though they've had hail damage, I will remember it's you I love and not the package outside. And when I think I don't love you any more because all the feeling has disappeared, I won't panic. I'll expect these times will come—and I'll stick it out and do everything it takes to keep us together until the feelings come back again. This includes going for "help" if neither of us knows what to do. (A marriage counselor? OK, for us, I'll do it.)

To love—To tell you "I love you" every single day because women have a very short memory in this category. And to remember that "Gee, you are more beautiful to me now than you've ever been" is equal to at least three "I love you's." Sharing a private joke or a knowing wink across a crowded room may be worth ten "I love you's." And "I'm sorry" and "I forgive you" are equal to at least a hundred.

And to cherish—I'll remember that you need to be treated as a piece of rare china. This means I won't get out of the pickup, walk toward the house, look back to see you still sitting there waiting, and say, "What's the matter, Babe, your arm broken? Can't get the door open?"

From this day forward—That means from now to Eternity. Forever. To commit to something like Eternity I will need supernatural strength. Because no human being can ever fulfill all the needs of my heart, not even you, I will remember I'm always loved by Someone. When you turn your back to me in the night, I will hang in there because I know I'm accepted by a Savior who never fails me. And when I act like a jerk, and I fail at loving you, remember His love will never fail you either. And with the Lord guiding us, there can always be fresh starts.

'Til death do us part—This means the only way I will ever leave you is if one of us dies from sickness or is killed by a tragic accident. Unless one of those two things occurs, we won't separate. I will never walk out and leave you a note telling you to "Get an attorney. It's over." This is the most binding contract we will ever make, and even though we are young, we both know that forever is a really, really long time. Someday we'll get old. And I want to be rocking next to you, holding love-weathered hands. Sweethearts, forever and always.

Well, Bubba, that about sums up what I took an entire book to write—at least from the man's point of view. You are young and in love, and I envy you a little. But not *too* much. Because I *really* like what I have—nearly twenty years after I married my eighteen-year-old groom. Just wait until you're middle-aged and know each other's faults and have weathered some major storms—and are still crazy in love. All I can say is that nothing we have ever worked to keep has been as well worth saving.

"This is it!" Adam exclaimed. "She is part of my own bone and flesh! Her name is 'woman' because she was taken out of a man." This explains why a man leaves his father and mother and is joined to his wife in such a way that the two become one person.

GENESIS 2:23–24, TLB

THIRTY-THREE

Back to the beach

We are on vacation again, and once again, I've had the exquisite pleasure of two hours alone. Alone, that is, except for my icy cold fruit drink, a gentle ocean breeze, the echo of waves splashing the shore, a pen and notebook, and—this time—the company of my old favorite book, Arthur Gordon's *A Touch of Wonder*. More and more I feel this writer and I are soul mates. I suspect we are both easily reduced to sentimental mush—and I have the feeling there aren't many of us around anymore. At the close of almost every chapter, I find myself inwardly shouting, *"I know! I feel that, too!"*

(By the way, in praise of "mushies," Golda Meir once said, "I have always felt sorry for people afraid of feeling, of sentimentality, who are unable to weep with their whole heart. Because those who do not know how to weep do not know how to laugh either."[1] I think she may be on to something.)

Anyway, I wonder if I might share with you a scene from this Sentimental Journey—this "fall in love with life" book? I'm dying to share it with someone, and the only other living thing nearby is a crab-looking critter preoccupied with catching the first wave out of here.

In the scene, Gordon is standing on a spot where the emerald ocean meets the glistening beach. He is lovingly, achingly watching his daughter—dressed in flowing white, barefoot and carrying a bouquet of sea oats—as she and her intended prepare to say their wedding vows. But before the "Will you's?" and "I do's" and "So be it's," the minister admonishes the young couple to pay careful attention to the laws of love.

"Real love," the minister says, "is caring as much about the welfare and happiness of your marriage partner as about your own. Real love is not total absorption in each other; it is looking outward in the same direction—together."

"All true," the author/father-of-the-bride thinks to himself. But as the seasoned father reflects upon his own marriage, his thoughts take a gut-wrenchingly honest turn.

"But you can't learn it from hearing it. You have to learn it by living it, and even then no one but a saint can apply more than fragments of it to his own marriage or his own life. All we can do, even the best of us, is try. And even then, the trying is hard."[2]

I read those words, and as I look out over the top of my tucked-up knees, I notice the seascape has already changed since last I glanced up. The sun has busied itself painting ripe nectarine strokes across the dunes. A white spray of gossiping seagulls vie for prey at ocean's edge, and a huge ship has lumbered into view. But as always, the waves are still lapping up the sand in their timeless rhythmic dance. The steady beat, the in and out of the tide, makes me think of the twenty years I've known the man who is my husband—years filled with reaching-outs, loving words, and tender touches.

"You have to learn it by living it."

Years full of failed attempts to communicate and clashes of anger, coupled with the eventual, inevitable determination to pick up the pieces and try again.

"And even then, the trying is hard."

I think of all the books I've read and the sermons and seminars I've heard on "How to Have a Happy Marriage." Always I close the books and walk away from these sorts of talks with the gnawing feeling that the well-intentioned authors and speakers must have it doubly hard. There *must* be times when the "experts"—the counselors, Ph.Ds, and esteemed seminary graduates—have to deliver their "ten principles of merry matrimony" on the heels of a heated exchange with their own beloved spouses. As for myself, there have been days over the past few months when I have sat down to write in praise of marriage, even as I swallowed lumps in my throat over a squabble Scott and I were having at the time. I still struggle to put into practice the joyous convictions in my heart. After all, we are so very human when it comes to carrying out the laws of love, especially the First-Corinthians-Thirteen-Agape type of love.

"No one but a saint can apply more than fragments of it to his own marriage or his own life."

And that, my friend, is the no-punches-pulled, most unadulterated truth about the inner workings of a marriage I've ever come across. With all the ups and downs and problems and failures, how have Scott and I made it thus far? I've written an entire book on the subject now, and still I haven't figured out exactly why or how. Some things—like our crazy, peculiar brand of love—are impossible to explain. They just are.

There are three things that are too amazing for me, four that I do not understand: the way of an eagle in the sky, the way of a snake on a rock, the way of a ship on the high seas, and the way of a man with a maiden.

PROVERBS 30:18–19

EPILOGUE

Note from a peculiar husband on the subject of his peculiar wife

For the better part of six months, Becky has been handing me chapters from this book to read at what seemed like every turn—under my nose while shaving, beside my morning coffee, on my pillow before I lay down at night—she even read one aloud as I was taking a shower. Some of the chapters made me laugh, some made me cry, some made me glad she didn't write everything she *could* have written.

But there was one chapter in this book that stood out because it showed the "Best of Becky." That was her chapter on looking at life from the most positive perspective—believing the best of God, of other people, of life in general. She is the only person I know who has faced her own failures and inadequacies and has experienced disappointment and hurt from other people, and yet she continues to brush herself off, get up, and try again to "go for the gold." I am honored and awed to be married to this lady.

One day a man named Richard passed my wife on the street. She only smiled and said, "Hello," to him. But he followed

Becky into a restaurant to tell her something that just about sums her up for me too. He said, "Ma'am, I just never met a woman quite like you."

Me either, Richard. Me either.

Notes

Introduction

1. Erma Bombeck, *A Marriage Made in Heaven or Too Tired for an Affair* (New York: Harper Collins, 1993), 256.

Chapter 7

1. Rafe VanHoy, "What's Forever For?" © 1978 Sony Tree Publishing Co., Inc.; all rights administered by Sony Music Publishing, 8 Music Square West, Nashville, TN 37203; all rights reserved and used by permission.

Chapter 9

1. Deb Frazier and Jan Winebrenner, *When a Leader Falls* (Minneapolis, Minn.: Bethany House, 1994).

Chapter 11

1. Jean Lush with Patricia H. Rushford, *Emotional Phases of a Woman's Life* (Tarrytown, N.Y.: Fleming H. Revell, 1987).

Chapter 15

1. Winston Churchill quoted in Alan Loy McGinnis's *The Romance Factor* (San Francisco: Harper & Row, 1982), 126.

Chapter 16

1. George Eliot, *Middle March* (1872), available from Signet of Penguin Books, New York.

Chapter 17

1. Arthur Gordon, *A Touch of Wonder,* "Interview with an Immortal" (New York: Fleming H. Revell, 1974), 63–68.

Chapter 18

1. Gary Paulsen, *Clabbered Dirt, Sweet Grass* (San Diego: Harcourt Brace & Co., 1992).
2. Interview with Gary Paulsen, *Writer's Digest,* July 1994.

Chapter 25

1. Fyodor Mikhailovich Dostoevsky, *The Idiot* (1868), quoted in *The International Thesaurus of Quotations,* Rhoda Thomas Tripp, compiler (New York: Harper & Row, 1987).
2. Mark Twain, *Notebook* (1935), *Thesaurus of Quotations*
3. Twain, *What Is a Man?* (1906) *Thesaurus of Quotations,.*

Chapter 28

1. Elizabeth Cody Newenhuyse, *Strong Marriages, Secret Questions* (Batavia, Ill.: Lion Publishing, 1987), 158.

Chapter 29

1. Madeleine L'Engle, *Two-Part Invention: The Story of a Marriage* (New York: Harper & Row, 1988), 232.

Chapter 30

1. Lewis B. Smedes, *Shame and Grace* (New York: Harper San Francisco & Zondervan Publishing House, 1993), 131.

Chapter 33

1. Quoted in Alan Loy McGinnis, *The Friendship Factor* (Minneapolis, Minn.: Augsburg Press, 1979).
2. Gordon, *A Touch of Wonder,* "Wedding by the Sea," 19–23.